Britain and the Arab–Israeli Conflict

London: H M S O

Researched and written by Reference Services, Central Office of Information.

© Crown copyright 1993
Applications for reproduction should be made to HMSO.
First published 1993

ISBN 0 11 701763 9

HMSO publications are available from:

HMSO Publications Centre
(Mail, fax and telephone orders only)
PO Box 276, London SW8 5DT
Telephone orders 071-873 9090
General enquiries 071-873 0011
(queuing system in operation for both numbers)
Fax orders 071-873 8200

HMSO Bookshops
49 High Holborn, London WC1V 6HB   071-873 0011
Fax 071-873 8200 (counter service only)
258 Broad Street, Birmingham B1 2HE   021-643 3740   Fax 021-643 6510
Southey House, 33 Wine Street, Bristol BS1 2BQ
0272 264306   Fax 0272 294515
9-21 Princess Street, Manchester M60 8AS   061-834 7201   Fax 061-833 0634
16 Arthur Street, Belfast BT1 4GD   0232 238451   Fax 0232 235401
71 Lothian Road, Edinburgh EH3 9AZ   031-228 4181   Fax 031-229 2734

HMSO's Accredited Agents
(see Yellow Pages)

and through good booksellers

Contents

Acknowledgments

The Central Office of Information would like to thank the Foreign and Commonwealth Office for its co-operation in compiling this book.

Introduction

Conflict between Arab and Jew in modern history dates back for more than a century, as Jewish Zionist ambitions increasingly clashed with emergent Arab nationalism. Since the declaration of the State of Israel in 1948 this conflict has on occasions posed a serious threat to world peace.

Efforts to find a just and durable settlement, based since 1967 on the 'land for peace' formula of United Nations Security Council Resolution 242 (see p. 16), have made some progress—notably the Egypt–Israel peace treaty of 1979, which resulted from the Camp David 'framework' agreements brokered by the United States the previous year (see p. 27). The agreements also sought to resolve the status of the Israeli-occupied territories and the rights of the Palestinian Arabs, but these problems have so far remained intractable.

Britain[1] and its European Community (EC) partners maintain that a lasting settlement can only be achieved through a compromise in which Israel recognises the right of the Palestinians to self-determination and the Arabs recognise Israel's right to exist within secure borders—in effect the exchange of territory for peace envisaged by UN Security Council Resolution 242.

This book outlines Britain's historical involvement in the Middle East, and its gradual administrative and military

---

[1] The term 'Britain' is used informally in this book to mean the United Kingdom of Great Britain and Northern Ireland; 'Great Britain' comprises England, Wales and Scotland.

disengagement from the region. It goes on to describe the evolution of Britain's policy towards the Arab–Israeli conflict and its diplomatic efforts, in unison with the other EC member states, towards a lasting peace settlement. Coverage concludes in April 1993.

Early British Policy

During the nineteenth century British policy aimed to preserve the Middle East region, which was largely within the Ottoman (Turkish) Empire, from domination by outside powers in order to protect communication routes to British India. From the early years of the twentieth century the discovery of oil—for commercial exploitation as a major source of energy—in southern Persia (Iran), Bahrain, Iraq, Saudi Arabia and Kuwait added a further dimension to Britain's interest in the region.

In order to deter interference with Indian shipping, the port of Aden[2] was occupied in 1839 by an expedition sent by the East India Company. At the 1878 Congress of Berlin it was agreed that Britain should take over control of Cyprus from the Turks in the face of a Russian threat to the integrity of the Ottoman Empire. Britain's occupation of Egypt in 1882 was continued until 1922 for the purpose of ensuring the neutrality of Egypt and the freedom of the Suez Canal[3] in the face of first French and later German threats to the area. Sudan came under British control in 1898. Among the coastal sheikdoms of the Gulf, Britain's influence was maintained through a series of treaties during the period.

[2] Situated in the south west of the Arabian peninsula, now part of Yemen. The colony was retained by Britain until 1967.

[3] The Suez Canal opened in 1869. Aware that it would add a new and most effective route to India, Britain had initially opposed its construction. Its importance was recognised in the Suez Canal Convention of 1888, signed by Austria-Hungary, France, Germany, Britain, Italy, the Netherlands, Russia, Spain and Turkey. The Convention made the defence of the Canal a special concern of all the signatory powers, who were to advise and concert on the measures necessary to maintain the freedom and security of navigation.

The First World War

Under strong German economic and political influence, the Ottoman Empire entered the first world war in 1914 on the side of the central European powers. Resistance in the Middle East devolved on Britain and France in collaboration with developing Arab nationalism. Britain was virtually obliged to seek Arab allies, both to protect the routes to India and to forestall the religious influence of the Islamic Ottoman Sultan on the Muslim subjects of the British Empire.

Britain undertook to support Arab struggles for independence from Ottoman suzerainty over large parts of the Middle East. The correspondence in 1915–16 between Sir Henry McMahon, British High Commissioner in Cairo (Egypt), and the Sherif Hussein of Mecca, who was offered British support for his ambitions of Arab statehood, was a precursor of the Arab revolt against the Turks in 1916. At the same time, under the 1916 Sykes–Picot agreement, Britain and France prepared for the post-war division of Middle Eastern Ottoman territories into British and French spheres of influence, albeit while still supporting areas of Arab independence.

Balfour Declaration

Although the dispersion (or Diaspora) of the Jews from Palestine dates from antiquity, Jewish communities kept alive the aspiration to a territorial centre. This intensified in the latter part of the nineteenth century as anti-semitism spread in Europe and Russia. Violent persecution stimulated Jewish emigration and gave impetus to the Zionist movement. The first World Zionist Congress in 1897 declared that: 'The aim of Zionism is to create for the Jewish people a home in Palestine secured by public law.' Between 1880 and 1914 Jewish settlement in Palestine almost quadrupled to about 90,000.

In sympathy with the Zionist cause, the British Government in 1917 issued the Balfour Declaration (see Documentation, p. 69) a move which remains the subject of historical debate and which angered Arab opinion. The Declaration stated that the Government viewed the establishment in Palestine of a national home for the Jewish people with favour. While it aimed to facilitate this objective, it also maintained that nothing should be done which might prejudice the civil and religious rights of existing non-Jewish communities in Palestine, or the rights and political status enjoyed by Jews in any other country.

Before the end of the war Britain had therefore given undertakings to both Arabs and Jews concerning Ottoman territories in the Middle East of which future Palestine formed a legally undefined part.[4] However, these undertakings fell short of promising either Arab or Jew a sovereign state in Palestine.

---

[4] For 400 years the Ottoman Empire had used neither the name 'Palestine' nor administrative divisions corresponding to those which would form the boundaries of the British Mandate.

League of Nations Mandates

The first world war ended in 1918 with the defeat of the central European powers and the disintegration of the Ottoman Empire. The post-war Covenant of the League of Nations[5] declared that 'Certain communities formerly belonging to the Turkish Empire have reached a stage of development where their existence as independent nations can be provisionally recognised subject to the rendering of administrative advice and assistance by a mandatory until such time as they are able to stand alone'.

In accordance with the decisions of the San Remo conference of April 1920, Britain received mandates for the territory of Palestine, the Kingdom of Iraq and the Amirate of Transjordan. France received mandates for Syria and the Lebanon. The terms of the mandates made it clear that they were of a temporary nature and were granted to facilitate the progressive development of the territories as independent states.

The Mandate for Palestine

The Mandate document (see Documentation, p. 69), approved by the League of Nations in June 1922, incorporated the Balfour Declaration committing Britain to secure the Jewish national home while protecting the non-Jewish population. Also in June 1922, in the light of Arab–Jewish clashes, the British Government issued the Churchill Memorandum (see Documentation, p. 73). This sought to reassure the Arabs that Britain did not intend that

[5] The League of Nations was established in 1920.

Palestine should become 'as Jewish as England is English' and that their language and culture would not be subordinated.

However, intercommunal conflict set the pattern of the history of the British Mandate. The Mandate Government had increasingly to protect the Arab population against the greater resources of the Jewish immigrants and their hunger, above all, for land.

By 1937 a Royal Commission on Palestine (the Peel Commission) was recommending partition into a Jewish and an Arab state as a solution to the problem (see Documentation, p. 76). However, the proposal was rejected, the British Government reaffirming its belief in a single state embracing both communities. This principle was reiterated in 1939, when a Government White Paper (see Documentation, p. 77) recommended restrictions on Jewish immigration, provoking Zionist hostility. Also unpopular among the Jewish population were the Land Transfers Regulations of 1940, aimed at protecting Arab land holdings against superior Jewish purchasing power. Such measures, particularly the immigration restrictions, encouraged anti-British Jewish violence and terrorism, even before the end of the second world war and while questions on the ultimate status of Palestine remained frozen.

The end of the second world war in 1945 signalled an increase in intercommunal strife. In 1945 independent Arab states (see p. 9) set up the Arab League, proclaiming their intention to give active support to Palestinian Arab aspirations. On the Jewish side, the traumatic experience of the Nazi Holocaust in Europe reinforced Zionist determination to secure a Jewish political entity in Palestine.

Jewish suffering under the Nazis won widespread sympathy for the Zionist cause, particularly in the United States, where official pressure and popular opprobrium was directed against Britain for its continuing attempts to enforce Jewish immigration restrictions. In Britain itself, the maintenance of large forces in Palestine to police the Mandate was unpopular.

Creation of Israel

By April 1947, Britain found the Mandate unworkable and submitted the problem to the new United Nations Organisation (UN).[6] At this stage there were some 1,200,000 Arabs and 600,000 Jews in Palestine. The UN General Assembly adopted Resolution 181 in November 1947, which provided for a 'Plan of Partition with Economic Union' (see Map 1, and Documentation, p. 82). This laid down steps for bringing both Arab and Jewish states to independence, with special arrangements for Jerusalem.

No progress had been made towards implementing the plan when Britain relinquished the Mandate on 14 May 1948 and the Jewish leadership proclaimed the State of Israel. Open warfare developed between the Jewish community and the independent Arab states, whose forces entered Palestine on 15 May. In the fighting, which continued intermittently until March 1949, Israeli forces not only secured virtually all of the territory allotted to the Jews under the UN partition plan but also took control of substantial additional areas.

Armistice agreements were signed by Israel with Egypt, Lebanon, Transjordan and Syria (but not Iraq) between February and July 1949. Israel surrendered areas of captured territory in southern Lebanon, northern Sinai and the Gaza Strip but was left in control of over two-thirds of the territory of Palestine (see Map 2).

[6] The United Nations was established in 1945 to maintain international peace and security. Britain has since then been one of five permanent members of the 15-member Security Council. The other permanent members are the United States, France, the People's Republic of China and Russia.

Independence of Arab States

Egypt had become a British protectorate at the outbreak of war with the Turks in 1914, and in 1922 was declared by the British Government to be an independent sovereign state. Negotiations to settle outstanding issues—including the securing of British imperial communications and the maintenance of British troops in the Suez Canal zone—resulted in the signature in August 1936 of the Anglo-Egyptian Treaty. In 1937 Egypt became a full member of the League of Nations.

For Iraq, the British Government considered by the end of the 1920s that the objectives of the Mandate had been achieved, and secured its termination in October 1932. Iraq was then admitted as a full member of the League, and the Anglo-Iraqi Treaty of Alliance, signed in 1930, came into effect.

In March 1946 Britain recognised the full sovereign independence of Transjordan. A treaty of alliance with Britain was made on the termination of the Mandate and a further treaty was concluded in March 1948. In 1950 the country became the Hashemite Kingdom of Jordan.

The French mandates in Syria and Lebanon, still in force when Germany occupied France in 1940, were brought to an end in 1943–44.

Developments to 1956

An important aspect of the 1948–49 war was the displacement of several hundreds of thousands of Arab Palestinians from Israeli-controlled areas. A large proportion remained concentrated in the Jordanian-held West Bank (territory lying west of the River Jordan—formally annexed by Jordan in 1950) and in the Egyptian-controlled Gaza Strip. Only some 150,000 Arabs remained within the extended borders of the new Israeli state, which initiated a massive programme of Jewish immigration and development.

In April 1950 Britain formally recognised the State of Israel. At the same time it stated that it recognised only the *de facto* authority exercised by Israel and Jordan over their respective sectors of Jerusalem, and that it did not regard the armistice lines between Israel and its neighbours as constituting definitive frontiers.

The Tripartite Declaration

A declaration was issued by Britain, France and the United States in May 1950. They recognised that the Arab states and Israel needed to maintain 'a certain level of armed forces for the purposes of assuring their internal security and their legitimate self-defence and to permit them to play their part in the defence of the area as a whole'. Applications for arms would be considered in the light of these principles.

The three governments affirmed their opposition to the development of an arms race between the Arab states and Israel and declared 'their deep interest in, and their desire to promote, the establishment and maintenance of peace and stability in the area and their unalterable opposition to the use of force or threat of force between any of the states in the area'. They also pledged that 'should they find that any of these states was preparing to violate frontiers or armistice lines' they would 'immediately take action, both within and outside the United Nations, to prevent such a violation'.

Relations between Israel and its Arab neighbours remained troubled, with outbreaks of violence along the armistice lines particularly from 1953 onwards. In general, the pattern was one of infiltration into Israel by irregular forces from territory controlled by Jordan and Egypt, followed at intervals by large-scale retaliation sorties by the Israeli army.

Arab Economic Blockade of Israel

From May 1948 the Arab states imposed an economic blockade of Israel. In particular, the Egyptian Government denied passage through the Suez Canal to Israeli shipping and to other shipping carrying 'strategic goods' to Israel. In defiance of a 1951 UN Security Council resolution, Egypt extended its restrictions in 1953 to cover foodstuffs and all other commodities 'likely to strengthen the war potential' of Israel.

The Suez Crisis

In Egypt, defeat in the 1948–49 war with Israel was a catalyst for revolution in 1952 and Colonel Nasser's takeover in 1954 (such revolutionary socialist and nationalist regimes coming to power in much of the Arab world in the 1950s and 1960s). Earlier, in 1951, the Egyptian Government had abrogated the 1936 treaty with Britain. An agreement with the new regime on the withdrawal of British forces from the Suez Canal zone was reached in 1954, but relations deteriorated as Egypt exerted its influence against the

Baghdad Pact[7] and turned to the Soviet communist bloc for arms supplies.

A month after the last British forces left Egypt in June 1956 in accordance with the 1954 agreement, Colonel Nasser announced the nationalisation of the agency controlling the operation of the Suez Canal. Britain, France and the United States maintained that the Egyptian act involved the arbitrary and unilateral seizure of an international agency and threatened the freedom and security of the Canal as guaranteed by the 1888 Convention. Subsequent negotiations to establish operating arrangements under an international system proved fruitless.

Outbreak of Hostilities

In October 1956 Israel launched an attack on Egypt in collusion, it later transpired, with Britain and France, which sought to repossess the Canal zone.

The sequence of events was as follows. On 29 October Israeli forces attacked Egyptian positions in the Gaza Strip and Sinai with the declared purpose of destroying commando bases. On the following day the British and French Governments issued 12-hour ultimatums to both Egypt and Israel demanding that both sides cease warlike actions and withdraw their troops from the immediate vicinity of the Suez Canal, thus anticipating Israeli possession

---

[7] In February 1955 Iraq and Turkey signed the Baghdad Pact providing for co-operation in matters of security and defence. The Pact was open for accession by any state 'actively concerned' with peace and security in the region. Between April and November 1955 Britain, Pakistan and Iran acceded to the agreement. Revolution in Iraq in 1958 put an end to Iraqi participation in the Pact. The other members, however, reaffirmed the alliance which was renamed the Central Treaty Organisation (CENTO) in 1959. CENTO was dissolved in September 1979 following the withdrawal of Iran, Pakistan and Turkey.

of Sinai. The ultimatums also requested that Egypt allow British and French forces be stationed temporarily on the Canal to separate the belligerents and safeguard shipping.

Egypt's rejection of the ultimatum was followed on 31 October by a British and French air offensive (launched from Cyprus) against Egyptian air bases and, on 5 November, by British and French paratroop and commando landings in the Canal zone— an operation which was opposed by the United States. Meanwhile, Israeli forces overran the whole of the Sinai peninsula.

Under pressure from the United States, a ceasefire was put into effect at midnight on 6–7 November, following which British and French forces were withdrawn and replaced by a United Nations Emergency Force. Israeli forces withdrew progressively up to March 1957.

The Suez episode was detrimental to British and French influence in the Middle East. It allowed the Soviet Union to fill the vacuum, promoting the radicalisation of Arab politics and supplying arms. This in turn drew the United States, with its powerful internal Jewish lobby, into the Middle East arena as the principal backer of Israel.

The Third Arab–Israeli War

Although Israel was restored to the borders established under the 1949 armistices, armed clashes between Arabs and Israelis continued in the decade following the 1956 Suez war, particularly along Israeli–Syrian border areas. Other sources of friction were the renewal in 1959 of Egypt's blockade of Israeli trade through the Suez Canal and the division of the waters of the River Jordan between Israel and the riparian Arab states.

The first Arab summit conference of 1964 led to the creation of the Palestine Liberation Organisation (PLO), with its own army. Later, in 1974, under Yasser Arafat's chairmanship it won wide international acceptance as the legitimate representative of the Palestinian people. Acting as an umbrella organisation for numerous and ideologically disparate Palestinian groups, the PLO adopted its Covenant pledging to eliminate Zionism in Palestine.

The Six-day War

Palestinian guerrilla incursions into Israel across the borders of Egypt, Jordan and Syria increased in the mid-1960s and were among the major contributory causes of the third Arab–Israeli war in June 1967. Others included Syrian shelling of Israeli villages in the Tiberias area and Colonel Nasser's claimed closure of the Straits of Tiran in May. As the likelihood of war increased, Arab and Israeli forces were mobilised and, on 5 June, the Israeli Air Force launched pre-emptive strikes against airfields in Egypt, Syria and Jordan, destroying virtually all the war planes of these countries on the first day of what subsequently became known as the Six-day War.

With the benefit of this air supremacy, Israel achieved a rapid victory over the Arab states. By the time hostilities ended in a ceasefire on 10 June, Israel had gained control of the Gaza Strip and Sinai peninsula from Egypt, the eastern (Arab) sector of Jerusalem and all of the Jordanian territory west of the River Jordan and, from Syria, the Golan Heights. By the end of the war Israeli forces were in occupation of an area more than three times greater than the territory of Israel at the outbreak of hostilities (see Map 3).

Arab reaction was characterised by a summit conference in the Sudanese capital of Khartoum in August 1967. The conference resolved to seek a political solution but also maintained that there would be no peace, recognition of, or negotiations with Israel. Israel stressed that a settlement of the Arab–Israeli conflict was dependent on direct talks with the surrounding Arab states to establish definitive boundaries which took account of Israel's legitimate security interests.

British View

Speaking on 17 June 1967, the Foreign Secretary, George Brown, said that the crisis had been 'a terrible warning of how miscalculations and misunderstandings can bring about an escalation of an international dispute to a flashpoint at which the international community is powerless to prevent an explosion'. Political problems following the war had to be tackled with restraint and statesmanship if the future was not to be worse than the past.

He maintained that the British Government had always opposed the use of force to solve disputes and supported the principle of territorial integrity and political independence of states.

Both of these principles were clearly stated in the United Nations Charter. Continuing, he said: 'It follows, therefore, that in the case of the Middle East problem it is not acceptable that solutions should be imposed by force. Accordingly, one contribution to a settlement must be the recognition that war should not lead to territorial aggrandisement.'

Mr Brown called on the international community to achieve a permanent solution. 'Justice and the facts of the situation demand that henceforth none of the countries of the area should feel threatened. They all have a right to security and it is in the interests of the international community as a whole to ensure this.'

United Nations Security Council Resolution 242

Peace moves continued at the United Nations and led eventually to the adoption of the British-sponsored Security Council Resolution 242 on 22 November 1967 (see Documentation, p. 87). It emphasised 'the inadmissibility of the acquisition of territory by war and the need to work for a just and lasting peace in which every state in the area can live in security'. The Resolution went on to affirm that the fulfilment of UN Charter principles required the establishment of peace in the Middle East based on the following principles:

—withdrawal of Israeli armed forces from territories occupied in the recent conflict; and

—'termination of all claims or states of belligerency and respect for and acknowledgement of the sovereignty, territorial integrity and political independence of every state in the area and their right to live in peace within secure and recognised boundaries free from threats or acts of force'.

It further affirmed the necessity for:

—guaranteeing freedom of navigation through international waterways in the area;

—achieving a just settlement of the refugee problem; and

—guaranteeing 'the territorial inviolability and political independence of every state in the area through measures including the establishment of demilitarised zones'.

The Resolution also provided for a special representative of the UN Secretary-General to visit the region and establish contacts with the states concerned in order to promote a peaceful settlement.

Resolution 242 was accepted by Israel and some Arab states, although on the basis of differing interpretations of the wording. Syria, Iraq and the PLO rejected it on the grounds that it treated the Palestinians only as a refugee problem.

Polarisation, 1967–73

Following the Six-day War, Israel made no immediate move to annex its conquests, which were placed under military administration, but it did merge the western (Israeli) and eastern (Arab) sectors of Jerusalem. The extension of its civil law to the whole city represented a *de facto* annexation. Only in 1980 did Israel claim *de jure* annexation with its 'Jerusalem Law', which proclaimed the entire city, whole and undivided, to be the eternal capital of Israel—a claim rejected by virtually the entire international community (see p. 29). The Israelis also began to build Jewish settlements in the occupied territories and were unwilling to allow the return of refugees.

In July 1969 President Nasser of Egypt forecast that a long 'war of attrition' would be needed to dislodge Israel from the occupied territories. Extremist Palestinian groups, especially the Popular Front for the Liberation of Palestine (PFLP) of Dr George Habash, resorted increasingly to terrorist activities.

The growth of guerrilla raids from Jordanian bases, including aircraft hijackings, led to Israeli retaliation into Jordan and raised tension between the Jordanian Government and the Palestinians. King Hussein of Jordan was committed to the principle of a political settlement with Israel, which the Palestinians believed would perpetuate Zionism. In the consequent confrontation in the 'Black September' of 1970, Jordanian forces decisively defeated and expelled the Palestinian resistance movement.

Meanwhile, diplomatic efforts to promote a peaceful settlement in the Middle East were maintained by the UN Security Council.

British Views on a Peace Settlement

Britain's view of the Arab–Israel problem and the nature of its settlement were set out by the Foreign and Commonwealth Secretary, Sir Alec Douglas-Home at Harrogate on 30 October 1970. He said that 'any such settlement must be based on two fundamental principles: the inadmissibility of the acquisition of territory by war, and the need for a just and lasting peace, in which every state in the area is guaranteed the right to live in security.'

Territorial Issues

A settlement, he continued, should establish a 'definitive agreement on territorial questions', which would answer both Israel's fear for its existence and 'Arab fear of Israeli expansionism'. This was why the balance between the provisions for Israeli withdrawal and secure and recognised boundaries was so important.

Sir Alec recognised that no 'outsider' could prescribe exactly where the boundaries should be and that they must first be agreed by the countries concerned if they were to be recognised. He believed, however, that:

— the international boundary that had long existed between Israel and Egypt should once again be recognised, subject to whatever arrangements might be made over the Gaza Strip;

— the boundary between Israel and Jordan should be based on the armistice lines which had existed before the 1967 war; and

— the boundary between Israel and Lebanon at that time should remain.

Regarding the Golan Heights, Sir Alec expected that once Syria accepted UN Security Council Resolution 242, 'the general principles governing the location of the other boundaries' would also govern that between Israel and Syria. On the special problem of Jerusalem, he considered that the only answer seemed to be some agreement providing for the freedom of access to the Holy Places and their protection.

Commitment to Peace

The second main pillar of the settlement would be binding commitments which the Arab countries and Israel would make to live at peace with one another. He said that these should include the establishment of a formal state of peace, and should cover an obligation on all states to refrain from any act or threat of hostility and to do all in their power to prevent the planning or conduct of any such acts on their territory.

A further clarification of Britain's view was given by the British delegate at the United Nations, Sir Colin Crowe, on 2 November 1970. On the guarantees for a settlement Sir Colin suggested that:

—the Security Council should endorse an agreement;

—as an internal guarantee, there should be a United Nations' presence both to supervise withdrawal and remain in the area thereafter;

—an important element might be the formation of demilitarised zones; and

—consideration should be given to any forms of external guarantee that might be proposed.

He added that there should also be guarantees for freedom of navigation through the Suez Canal, the Gulf of Aqaba and the Straits of Tiran. Britain recognised that a settlement which was fair and lasting would have to take account of Palestinian views, but only within the framework of Security Council Resolution 242.

The 1973 War and Aftermath

The fourth Arab–Israeli war broke out on 6 October 1973 (*Yom Kippur*—the holiest day in the Jewish year) when Egyptian and Syrian forces launched offensives across the Suez Canal and on the Golan front respectively. Syrian forces were joined by contingents from Jordan, Iraq and other Arab states. The declared war aims of Egypt and Syria were to recover the Arab territories lost to Israel in 1967 and restore the 'legitimate rights' of the Palestinians.

Hostilities broke out without warning, although they followed a spate of guerrilla and counter-terror operations in 1972–73. Also, in the summer of 1973, the United States had vetoed a UN Security Council resolution critical of Israel's continued occupation of Arab territory, helping to persuade Egypt and Syria to launch the war.

The ensuing bitter fighting, involving heavy losses on both sides, lasted some 20 days and was not effectively halted until three ceasefire resolutions had been adopted by the UN Security Council. By that time the Egyptian army had established itself along much of the eastern bank of the Suez Canal north of Ismailia (see Map 4) and held a narrow strip of Sinai amounting to some 1,300 sq km (500 sq miles) of territory. For their part, the Israelis had consolidated a successful counter-offensive across the Suez Canal in the southern sector, giving them control of about 1,300 sq km (500 sq miles) of Egyptian territory.

The Syrians achieved initial success against Israeli forces on the northern front, recapturing much of the Golan Heights lost in the 1967 war. However, they were checked and driven back by an Israeli counter-offensive, so that when a ceasefire came into effect they had surrendered their initial gains and lost a further 800 sq km (300 sq miles) of territory.

The Security Council's first ceasefire resolution (338) was proposed jointly by the United States and the Soviet Union, reflecting their concern that the conflict might escalate into a broader confrontation. Adopted on 22 October, the Resolution called for an immediate ceasefire and implementation of Resolution 242 in all its parts, and decided that immediate negotiations should be initiated 'aimed at establishing a just and durable peace in the Middle East' (see Documentation, p. 88).

In the light of continued fighting, a second joint US–Soviet resolution was adopted on 23 October repeating the call for a ceasefire. A third resolution, adopted on 25 October, authorised the establishment of a United Nations Emergency Force (UNEF) to be sent to the Suez front.

A ceasefire agreement was signed by Egypt and Israel, under United Nations auspices, on 11 November 1973. A peace conference under joint US–Soviet chairmanship was convened in December 1973 in Geneva, but the PLO was not invited and Syria refused to attend. The conference was adjourned inconclusively in January 1974.

British Position

In the years preceding the war Britain had provided limited and balanced amounts of armaments to both Israel and the Arab states. At the outbreak of hostilities in October 1973 the British

Government called for a ceasefire and immediately suspended arms supplies to the battlefield.

Defending the arms embargo, Sir Alec Douglas-Home said in mid-October that it would be kept under continuous review and would be reconsidered if, at any stage, the existence of Israel appeared to be at risk. The continued existence and prosperity of Israel as a state was one of the cardinal points of British policy towards the Middle East, and the British Government was determined that the State of Israel should continue to exist within secure frontiers.

Britain unreservedly supported the Security Council's case for an immediate ceasefire and the subsequent measures adopted to ensure its effectiveness. The Government reiterated, at the end of October, that a way had to be found to reconcile Israel's requirement for security with the demand of its neighbours for the recovery of their territory.

European Community View

In a declaration on 5 November, Britain and its European Community (EC) partners[8] expressed the firm hope that negotiations would at last begin for 'the restoration of a just and lasting peace through the application of Security Council Resolution 242 in all its parts'. They believed that such negotiations should take place in the framework of the United Nations and they declared themselves ready to do all in their power to contribute to a comprehensive solution.

[8] Britain became a full member of the European Community on 1 January 1973. For further information see *Britain in the European Community* (Aspects of Britain: HMSO, 1992).

Disengagement Agreements

A feature of the negotiations during 1974 and 1975, broadly under the aegis of UN Security Council Resolution 338 and leading to military disengagement agreements between Israel on the one hand and Egypt and Syria on the other (see Map 4), was the key diplomatic role played by the United States, and in particular by Secretary of State Henry Kissinger.

A related factor was concern over the use of the 'oil weapon' by Arab oil-exporting countries in order to bring pressure to bear on the Western industrialised powers. At the time of the 1973 war, use of this weapon took the form of an embargo on supplies to the United States and the Netherlands, as open supporters of Israel, and restrictions on supplies to other developed countries. Subsequently, there were large oil price rises which had serious consequences for the international monetary system.

Britain welcomed the 1974 disengagement agreements signed by Israel with Egypt and with Syria as important steps towards a peace settlement. Accordingly, the Government decided to lift the suspension of military supplies to the battlefield countries, although requests for arms remained subject to careful scrutiny.

A further disengagement agreement between Egypt and Israel was negotiated with the help of the United States in September 1975. However, most other Arab states opposed this agreement as a surrender to US and Israeli interests which ignored the Palestinian cause.

Palestinian Question

During 1974 the PLO made considerable political progress. Resolution 3236, adopted by the United Nations General

Assembly in November, stressed the inalienable rights of the Palestinian people in Palestine, including:

— the right to self-determination without external interference; and

— the right to national independence and sovereignty.

Resolution 3237 accorded the PLO observer status at the UN.

Equally important was the Arab League summit in Rabat in October at which Arab leaders, including King Hussein of Jordan, recognised the PLO as the sole legitimate representative of the Palestinian people in all territory to be liberated from Israel.

British Attitude

Britain accepted that a Middle East settlement, based on UN Security Council Resolutions 242 and 338, should also provide a means whereby the Palestinian people could exercise their legitimate political rights. Such rights, however, had to be wholly compatible with the continued and assured existence of Israel as a state.

Speaking at the UN Security Council in June 1976, the British representative, Ivor Richard, called for a willingness on all sides to compromise. The Palestinians, he said, had to accept the reality of Israel's existence as recognised by the majority of UN states. For their part, the Israelis needed to recognise the rights of the Palestinian people and to accept that Palestinian nationalist sentiment had to be taken into account in a settlement.

In a speech in October 1977 the Prime Minister, James Callaghan, emphasised both the necessity of a settlement that guaranteed Israel's existence and security, and the need to solve the Palestinian problem 'by setting up a homeland of some kind for the Palestinian Arabs'. This view had been affirmed by Britain's Community partners in an earlier statement by the European Council in June 1977.

Egyptian–Israeli Rapprochement

International efforts during 1977 to reconvene the Geneva peace conference culminated in a joint Soviet–United States statement on 1 October outlining the principles and objectives for a full Arab–Israeli settlement. However, these peace moves were pre-empted by the historic visit of President Sadat of Egypt to Israel in November, the first official visit by an Arab head of state to Israel since its foundation.

The visit was the more surprising since, in May 1977, the Israeli Labour Party, which had ruled Israel since the inception of the state, had been replaced in government by the right-wing *Likud* party. *Likud* opposed any territorial concessions and had immediately begun an ambitious settlement-building programme in the occupied territories.

Addressing the Israeli Parliament in an appeal for peace, President Sadat explicitly accepted the existence of Israel as a Middle East state. However, he insisted on complete Israeli withdrawal from the occupied territories, including East Jerusalem, and on recognition of the rights of the Palestinians. The Egyptian initiative was welcomed by Britain and its European Community partners and by the United States, but was opposed by Syria, Libya, Algeria, South Yemen and the PLO, which formed a 'front for resistance and confrontation'.

In December Israel put forward its own proposals for a peace settlement, involving gradual withdrawal from Sinai but only limited provision for Palestinian autonomy in the West Bank and Gaza Strip.

Further impetus towards a peaceful solution was checked in March 1978 when a Palestinian guerrilla raid on Israel was immediately followed by a large-scale Israeli invasion of southern Lebanon, designed to secure Israel's northern border against Palestinian incursions. However, the deployment of a United Nations peacekeeping force in southern Lebanon and the withdrawal of Israeli forces by mid-June facilitated efforts by the United States to bring about a resumption of direct Egyptian–Israeli negotiations.

Camp David Accords

A summit meeting was held between President Sadat of Egypt and Prime Minister Begin of Israel at Camp David (near Washington) in September 1978, with President Carter of the United States acting as intermediary.

The negotiations resulted in the signature of two 'framework' agreements. One provided for the conclusion of an Egyptian–Israeli peace treaty involving a staged withdrawal from Sinai (see Map 4). The other dealt with an overall Middle East settlement, stipulating that the Palestinian inhabitants of the West Bank and Gaza Strip should obtain 'full autonomy' during a transitional period of five years involving the establishment of a 'self-governing authority'. Israel would keep a military presence on the West Bank as a security measure.

Contentious issues which remained unresolved under the accords included Israel's continued settlement-building in the occupied territories and the status of Jerusalem.

Egypt–Israel Treaty

Further mediation efforts by the United States resulted in the signature in Washington by Egypt and Israel of the first-ever

Arab–Israeli peace treaty on 26 March 1979. The treaty provided for:

—an end to the state of war between the two countries;

—a phased Israeli withdrawal from Sinai over a three year period;

—agreed security arrangements involving the establishment of limited-force zones and the stationing of United Nations forces in border areas;

—the normalisation of diplomatic and other relations;

—the right of free passage through the Suez Canal for Israeli ships and cargoes;

—recognition of the Straits of Tiran and the Gulf of Aqaba as international waterways by both countries;

—the termination of economic boycotts and discriminatory barriers to the free movement of people and goods; and

—the start of negotiations on the implementation of the Camp David framework agreement relating to Palestinian autonomy and the establishment of a self-governing authority within one month of the ratification of the peace treaty.

British Reaction

Speaking on 27 March 1979, the Prime Minister said that peace between Egypt and Israel for the first time in 30 years was 'something at which the whole world should rejoice'. However, Mr Callaghan cautioned that Britain regarded it 'as essential that we should move on from here to a comprehensive peace settlement that will engage the other Arab states and give the Arabs in Palestine...the opportunity of a secure future for themselves, as well as securing peace for Israel'.

Arab Hostility

In the Arab world the price paid by Egypt for its signature of the treaty with Israel was political ostracism, the majority of Arab states imposing an economic and political boycott. In addition, Egypt was suspended from membership of several international organisations, in particular the Arab League, Islamic Conference Organisation and Organisation of Arab Petroleum Exporting Countries.

Treaty Implementation

Diplomatic relations between Israel and Egypt were established in February 1980. Despite tensions—engendered by Israel's extension of control over Jerusalem in 1980,[9] by its bombing of an Iraqi nuclear reactor[10] and effective annexation of the Golan Heights in 1981[11] and by deadlock over the issue of Palestinian autonomy—the

---

[9] In July 1980 Israel passed a law declaring that a united Jerusalem was the capital of Israel. Britain voted in favour of a UN Security Council resolution, adopted in August, censuring Israel for the legislation. The United States abstained in the vote. Britain maintained that Israeli rights in East Jerusalem—occupied by Israel's forces in the 1967 war—did not extend beyond those of an occupying power, pending an agreed solution on the city's future.

[10] In June 1981 Israeli aircraft bombed an Iraqi nuclear reactor on the outskirts of Baghdad. The UN Security Council adopted unanimously a resolution comdemning the Israeli action as being 'a clear violation of the Charter of the United Nations and the norms of international conduct'. It also called upon Israel to refrain from such acts or threats in the future.

[11] Israel extended its law, jurisdiction and administration to occupied Syrian territory in the Golan Heights on 14 December 1981. The UN Security Council unanimously declared Israel's action to be 'null and void' and 'without international effect'. A statement by the European Community deplored the action as 'tantamount to annexation' and contrary to international law.

In Britain's view the Golan Heights belonged to Syria and were subject to the principles emphasised in Security Council Resolution 242. The Government could not accept any unilateral initiative by Israel to change the territory's status.

Israeli withdrawal from Sinai was completed in April 1982 in accordance with the timetable laid down in the peace treaty.

Troops of an international peacekeeping force outside the United Nations framework (the Sinai Multinational Force and Observers), including a British contingent, were deployed along the reinstated international border between Egypt and Israel.

Palestinian Autonomy Issue

Against a background of continuing Israeli settlement-building in the West Bank and opposition to further territorial concessions to the Arabs, progress in negotiations on Palestinian autonomy was not forthcoming. Egypt regarded autonomy as a right of the Palestinians under international law and as a step towards independence. Israel saw it as a concept applying to people, not land, subject to Israeli domestic law and offering only a limited range of powers to the Palestinians. Areas such as defence and foreign relations were excluded.

Jordan and the Palestinians themselves refused any involvement with the talks. The PLO said that it would not relinquish its long-term aim of a democratic, secular state embracing all races and creeds, but would accept an independent Palestinian state in any part of former mandated Palestine from which Israel withdrew.

Israel, however, maintained that it would never accept a Palestinian state in the West Bank and Gaza. Increasingly violent Palestinian opposition to Israeli rule was accompanied by widespread and open support for the PLO, with which Israel refused to negotiate.

Further talks between Egypt and Israel on the issue of autonomy were suspended following the Israeli invasion of Lebanon (see p. 37).

The 1980 European Initiative

The need to resolve the Arab–Israeli conflict appeared ever more imperative at the end of the 1970s, as tension in the Middle East increased following the Iranian Islamic revolution and the Soviet invasion of Afghanistan.

Britain continued to believe that, while the principles of UN Security Council Resolution 242 remained the basis for peace in the region, the Palestinians had to be fully involved in any settlement and be able to participate in its negotiation. This view was reflected in a major policy statement by the European Community member states on 13 June 1980.

The Venice Declaration

The European Council's declaration on the Middle East (see Documentation, p. 88) included the following principles:

—the recognition and implementation of the right to existence and security of all the states in the region, including Israel, and justice for all the peoples, which implied the recognition of the legitimate rights of the Palestinian people;

—United Nations guarantees for a peace settlement, in which the EC member states would be prepared to participate;

—a just solution to the Palestinian refugee problem and the exercise by the Palestinians of their right to self-determination;

—the application of the above principles to all the parties including the Palestinian people, and to the PLO which would have to be associated with the negotiations;

—the rejection of any unilateral initiative designed to change the status of Jerusalem;

—the need for Israel to put an end to the territorial occupation which it had maintained since the conflict of 1967 (the Israeli settlements in the occupied territories constituted a serious obstacle to the peace process and were illegal under international law); and

—the renunciation of force or the threat of force by all parties.

British Statements

On 16 June the Prime Minister, Margaret Thatcher, said that the European Council had decided to make contact with all the parties in order to ascertain their positions (see below) and that Community diplomatic activity over the next few months was intended to be complementary to the Camp David process on which the United States, Egypt and Israel were still engaged.

Mrs Thatcher declared that, while Britain could not recognise the PLO as the sole representative of the Palestinian people, the reality of the situation was that there would not be a comprehensive settlement unless the PLO was associated with it. Likewise, 'just as the Israeli people will have to accept the legitimate rights of the Palestinian people, so the Palestinian people, including the PLO, will have to accept Israel's right to exist behind secure boundaries and be prepared to guarantee those boundaries.'

In July 1980 the Foreign and Commonwealth Secretary, Lord Carrington, noted that the Venice Declaration was criticised by Israel and by the United States for its reference to the PLO. He reiterated that, although the PLO would have to be associated with the negotiations, this did not constitute official recognition of the organisation. Rather it reflected the belief among EC member states that the PLO enjoyed considerable Palestinian support, both in the occupied territories and elsewhere.

Lord Carrington emphasised that 'unacceptable PLO policies and actions' could not be condoned and that the Venice Declaration had made it clear that the PLO had to accept the principles of a negotiated settlement including Israel's right to exist. Pointing out that Israel also had to modify its position, Lord Carrington said that the continuing expansion of settlements in the occupied territories made the achievement of peace much more difficult. Britain's fundamental commitment to Israel did not and could not extend to its 'actions as an occupying power'.

He stressed that the European Community initiative was complementary to the Camp David peace process, which Britain continued to support.

Follow-up Consultations

In July 1980 the President of the EC Council of Ministers undertook a consultation mission to the Middle East. After considering his report, the European Council said in December that the mission had confirmed that the principles of the Venice Declaration incorporated the 'essential elements for a comprehensive, just and lasting settlement to be negotiated by the parties concerned'.

The Council resolved to continue the positive process of consultation and inquiry, exploring ideas on key issues such as troop withdrawal, Palestinian self-determination, security in the region and the status of Jerusalem.

Peace Plans, 1981–82

In October 1981 President Sadat of Egypt was assassinated by Muslim extremists. His successor, President Mubarak, vowed to continue his policies, at the same time expressing approval of the European initiative and of Saudi Arabian peace proposals.

Saudi Peace Plan

In August 1981 Crown Prince (later King) Fahd of Saudi Arabia proposed an eight-point peace plan providing, in particular, for Israeli withdrawal from the Arab territories occupied in 1967 and the rise of an independent Palestinian state with Jerusalem as its capital. In addition, it called for the right of states to live in peace to be assured, thereby implying Israel's right to exist.

Lord Carrington welcomed both the implicit recognition and the indication of Saudi support for a negotiated settlement. There was considerable common ground between the plan and the Venice Declaration, to which Britain remained committed as a framework on which Middle East peace could eventually be built.

At the same time Britain recognised the achievements of the Camp David process and believed that the United States had to continue playing a central role in the peace effort.

United States Initiative

In September 1982 President Reagan of the United States announced a fresh initiative. The President said that the Arabs should recognise Israel's legitimacy but acknowledged that the Palestinian question was more than one of refugees.

The United States, he said, opposed both a Palestinian state in the West Bank and Gaza and continued Israeli sovereignty. It held that self-government by the Palestinians of the West Bank in association with Jordan offered the best chance for a just and durable peace. He added that Jerusalem should remain undivided, but its final status should be settled through negotiations.

The basis of this approach was that resolution of the conflict should involve the exchange of territory for peace, as enshrined in UN Security Council Resolution 242 and subsequently incorporated in the Camp David accords.

The Israeli Government rejected the initiative but the British Foreign and Commonwealth Secretary, Francis Pym (who replaced Lord Carrington in April 1982), described it as positive and constructive. Mr Pym added that the plan was 'very close to the ideas and opinions being expressed by Britain and the other European countries for a year or two now'.

Arab League Proposals

The Arab League summit meeting at Fez in September 1982 adopted an eight-point plan for Middle East peace, essentially reiterating the Saudi proposals of a year earlier. Again, in calling for the UN Security Council 'to guarantee peace among all states of the region, including the Palestinian state', the Arabs appeared to accept Israel's right to exist.

European Community View

In response to the United States and Arab initiatives, Britain and its EC partners called for 'a similar expression of a will to peace on the part of Israel'.

In a speech in November 1982 Mr Pym said that the term 'self-determination' which Britain and the other member states had used regarding Palestinian rights had been much misunderstood— not least in Israel, where it was taken to imply a Palestinian state hostile to Israeli interests. He explained: 'What we mean by it is that circumstances must be created in which the Palestinian people, through a choice of their own, can express their political aspirations and sustain their political identity. Clearly this expression of identity could take various constitutional forms. President Reagan's proposal for self-government in association with Jordan is one. A state is obviously another.' It would be illogical for the EC member states to rule out the latter, having supported the Palestinians' right to choose.

He added that, in Britain's view, Palestinian self-determination, far from being incompatible with Israeli security, was 'an essential part of a just and lasting peace'.

Israeli Invasion of Lebanon, 1982

The transplantation to Lebanon of Palestinian activists, after their forcible expulsion from Jordan in September 1970 (see p. 18), heightened Israel's concern over the security of northern Galilee. Palestinian guerrillas operated increasingly freely amid the collapse of central government authority which accompanied the 1975–76 civil war in Lebanon.

Israel responded by making direct attacks on Palestinian guerrilla bases in southern Lebanon—particularly in 1978, as a consequence of which a UN peacekeeping force (UN Interim Force in Lebanon—UNIFIL) was deployed—and by maintaining a buffer zone under the control of Lebanese Christian forces (who were hostile to the PLO) immediately to the north of the border. At the same time, Israel warned that it would not tolerate any move into southern Lebanon by the Syrian-dominated Arab Deterrent Force stationed in Lebanon from the end of the 1975–76 civil war.

Israeli Invasion

In July 1981 there was an escalation of fighting, which included Palestinian shelling of Israeli border settlements and an air raid by Israeli aircraft on the Lebanese capital of Beirut. A ceasefire was negotiated by the United States between the PLO and Israel. However, in early June 1982, in response to the attempted assassination of the Israeli ambassador to Britain, Israel invaded Lebanon (although the PLO was not responsible for the assassination attempt).

Lebanon's Borders

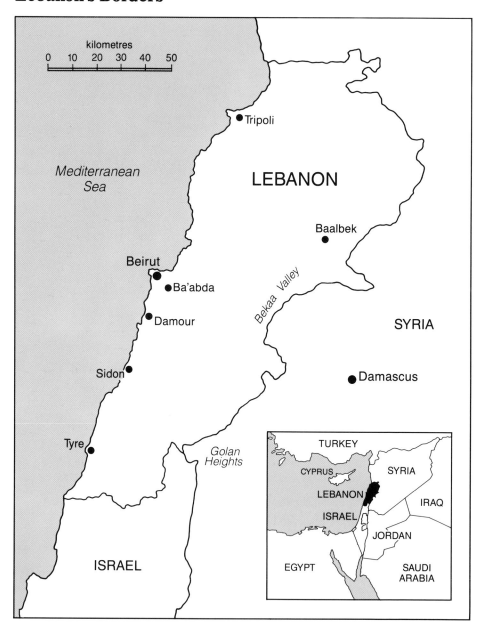

Within a few days the Israelis had occupied the entire southern Lebanon and reached the outskirts of Beirut, dispersing the PLO military presence and clashing with Syrian air and ground forces. With Britain's support, the UN Security Council and the European Community condemned the invasion and called on Israel to withdraw to the internationally recognised boundaries of Lebanon. Britain regarded Israel's invasion and occupation as a violation of Lebanon's sovereignty and did not accept Israeli claims to be acting in self-defence. Rejecting international demands, Israel maintained its occupation and its military pressure on Palestinian forces in Beirut.

PLO Departure from Beirut

In mid-August, after lengthy negotiations, the United States special envoy, Philip Habib, achieved an agreement between the Lebanese and Israeli Governments and the PLO. The plan provided for a ceasefire by all forces in Lebanon and for the departure of the PLO leadership and its forces from west Beirut and from Lebanon by early September. The PLO's departure for various Arab countries was overseen by the Lebanese armed forces assisted by a temporary multinational force comprising United States, French and Italian troops.

Throughout Mr Habib's negotiations, Britain had voiced the hope that the outcome would be successful and peaceful. Welcoming the agreement, the Foreign and Commonwealth Secretary, Mr Pym, said on 20 August that 'a major war in Beirut' had been averted.

Israeli Advance into West Beirut

On 14 September the Maronite Christian President-elect of Lebanon was assassinated. The following day, in violation of the ceasefire agreement negotiated by Mr Habib, Israeli troops advanced into Muslim west Beirut. The UN Security Council unanimously condemned the Israeli incursion and reiterated its call for 'strict respect for Lebanon's sovereignty, territorial integrity, unity and political independence'.

The British representative at the UN, Sir John Thomson, said that Israel 'had no right to arrogate to itself the power of intervention in the capital and territory of a neighbouring state', or 'to take the law into its own hands in someone else's country'. He continued: 'It is incumbent on all involved in the tragic situation in Lebanon to observe the greatest restraint and exercise prudence at this time of tension. A satisfactory situation can be achieved only when Israel withdraws its forces... and when all other foreign troops except any authorised by the Lebanese Government also withdraw.'

Sabra and Chatila Massacre

The Israeli Government responded to international criticism of its occupation of Beirut by announcing that it would not withdraw until all remaining arms caches and armed terrorist forces had been rooted out.

During 17 and 18 September it became apparent that Israeli military authorities had authorised Lebanese Christian militia groups to enter and search the Palestinian refugee camps of Sabra and Chatila and that a massacre of some 2,000 civilians had subsequently taken place. Reflecting UN Security Council reaction on 19 September, Mrs Thatcher referred to the massacre an an act of 'sheer barbarism which must bring total condemnation on its perpetrators'.

In a statement on 20 September, Britain and its European Community partners demanded the immediate withdrawal of

Israeli forces from west Beirut. They also sought the earliest possible withdrawal of all foreign forces except those authorised by the Government of Lebanon, whose authority should be fully reestablished over all its national territory. The statement added that the tragic events in Lebanon had once again demonstrated that the Middle East could enjoy true peace and lasting stability only through 'a comprehensive settlement to be concluded with the participation of all parties'.

Israel denied responsibility for the massacre but instituted a judicial inquiry, which was critical of government ministers and officials.

Israeli Withdrawal

In response to an appeal by the Lebanese Government, a strengthened multinational force of French, United States and Italian troops returned to Beirut in September as Israel began pulling back its forces. A small British contingent joined the force in February 1983. However, during 1983, internal security and political conditions in Lebanon deteriorated. Having become embroiled in Lebanese factional fighting and the target of terrorist attacks by fundamentalist elements, the multinational force was redeployed early in 1984.

An accord, signed by Lebanon and Israel in May 1983, was abrogated by the Lebanese Government under Syrian pressure in 1984. In January 1985 the Israeli Government decided on a unilateral staged withdrawal from Lebanon, which was completed in June. However, the Israelis established a self-declared security zone inside southern Lebanon to deter the resumption of Palestinian guerrilla operations.

The Mid-1980s

Overshadowed by the political and security situation in Lebanon, the United States and Arab peace initiatives of September 1982 did not sustain momentum. Developments in the mid-1980s centred largely on Jordan and its relationship with the PLO, on the problem of terrorism and on growing support for the idea of an international conference on the Middle East.

Jordan and the PLO

From 1983 Britain supported the ultimately unsuccessful efforts by King Hussein of Jordan to reach a common negotiating position with the PLO.

Although the Palestine National Council rejected President Reagan's peace initiative, it endorsed the concept of a future confederal relationship between Jordan and a Palestinian entity. In February 1985 Jordan and the PLO reached agreement on a plan calling for a negotiated Middle East settlement based on the exchange of territory for peace. It proposed:

—Israeli withdrawal from the West Bank and Gaza;

—the subsequent incorporation of those territories into a confederation with Jordan; and

—an international conference attended by the five permanent members of the UN Security Council and a joint Jordanian–Palestinian delegation.

However, conflicting interpretations quickly emerged between the two sides over the agreement. At the same time, Yasser Arafat's leadership of the PLO came under increasing challenge from hard-line elements within the organisation (mostly backed by Syria) which opposed any compromise on established PLO policy principles. In early 1986 King Hussein announced that Jordan was unable to continue to co-ordinate politically with the PLO leadership.

Terrorism and Reprisals

From 1984 to 1986 the attention of Western governments was focused primarily on the problem of terrorism related to the Middle East conflict. Some of the main incidents are described below.

Britain severed diplomatic relations with Libya in 1984 after a policewoman was killed by a shot fired from the Libyan embassy in London. In 1985 a United States airliner was hijacked to Beirut and was released only as a consequence of an exchange of Lebanese Shia Muslim detainees held by Israel.

In October of that year Israel carried out a bombing raid on the PLO headquarters in Tunis, capital of Tunisia. This was in retaliation for terrorist attacks on Israeli citizens, most recently in Cyprus. Britain supported the UN Security Council resolution condemning the Israeli raid. Although the British Government condemned any terrorist act anywhere in the world, it could not accept as valid the reasons put forward by Israel for its action.

Also in October, Palestinian extremists hijacked an Italian cruise ship—the *Achille Lauro*—in the Mediterranean, murdering a United States citizen before they surrendered. In November 1985 an Egyptian aircraft was hijacked to Malta and, in December, gunmen fired on the ticket counters of Israel's national airline at Rome and Vienna airports.

In April 1986, in response to a terrorist attack aimed at US servicemen in Berlin, United States aircraft (some of them operating from bases in Britain) bombed targets in Libya. In September Jews in a synagogue in the Turkish city of Istanbul were gunned down and a United States aircraft was hijacked to Pakistan. All these attacks and counter-attacks caused heavy, civilian casualties.

The British Government broke off diplomatic relations with Syria in November 1986, following the production of evidence of official Syrian support for terrorist activity in Britain. Support for Britain's action was expressed by its European Community partners and by the United States, which adopted sanctions against the Syrian Government. Relations were not restored until November 1990.

Western Hostages in Lebanon
During this period Western nationals, including some British citizens, became targets for abduction as hostages by Islamic fundamentalist extremists operating in Lebanon, particularly Beirut. Britain refused at all times to bargain with the kidnappers, maintaining its policy of making no concessions under duress to terrorists or their sponsors.

Although many of the hostages suffered long periods of captivity and deprivation in Lebanon, most had been released by the end of 1991, their kidnappers achieving nothing.

Diplomatic Moves

In January 1987 the Foreign and Commonwealth Secretary, Sir Geoffrey Howe, restated Britain's view of the requirements for a Middle East settlement. Five wars and 40 years of suffering had shown that there were no victories to be won except when each side recognised the strength as well as the legitimacy not of its own but of the other's position.

Israel, he said, was there to stay and had a right to security within recognised boundaries. At the same time, the Palestinians could not be wished away. Real peace would not be possible 'until Israel is freely accepted by the Palestinians whose future is at stake in any negotiated settlement ... until the Palestinians are permitted to exercise their right to self-determination ... until representatives of the Palestinians take part in negotiations ... and until those representatives ... in turn commit themselves unequivocally to repudiate violence and accept Israel's rights'.

Reaffirming that Britain and its European Community partners would continue to be active in promoting negotiations, Sir Geoffrey said that there was a growing consensus in the region that an international conference, properly managed, could be constructive. However, he recognised that such a conference had to be put to good use and not turned into a forum for 'ritual rhetoric'.

Commenting on the occupied territories, Sir Geoffrey said that the EC member states had, during Britain's presidency of the Community in the latter half of 1986, strongly reminded Israel of its obligations as an occupying power to respect human rights. They had increased their aid programme to the occupied territories and provided more resources to the United Nations Relief and Works Agency (UNRWA).[12]

[12] The UNRWA was founded in 1949 to bring assistance to Palestinian Arab refugees and to help them become self-supporting. Its mandate has repeatedly been renewed. Britain is one of the major donors to the UNRWA, providing some £6 million in 1992–93.

European Community Statement

Britain and the other EC member countries issued a statement in February 1987, marking the first major European initiative on the Middle East since the Venice Declaration of 1980 (see p. 31).

In their statement the Twelve reiterated their profound conviction that the search for peace remained a fundamental objective. They declared that they were in favour of an international peace conference to be held under the auspices of the United Nations— with the participation of all the parties concerned and of any party able to make a direct and positive contribution to the restoration and maintenance of peace and to the region's economic and social development. The Community member states would endeavour, collectively and individually, to make an active contribution to bringing the position of the parties concerned closer together.

Without prejudging future political solutions, the Twelve further expressed their wish to see an improvement in the living conditions of the inhabitants of the occupied territories.

The Community had for the first time offered united political support for the principle of an international conference in the hope that it would inject momentum into the peace process, the stagnation of which it regarded as dangerous.

Israeli Position

Israel at this time was governed by a national unity coalition between the Labour and *Likud* parties. The Labour Party considered that Israel should be prepared to make territorial concessions, consistent with its security requirements, in return for a peace treaty with Jordan. It also advocated a freeze on settlement activity in occupied areas of dense Palestinian population. In contrast,

Israel, Palestine and the Arabs, from 1947

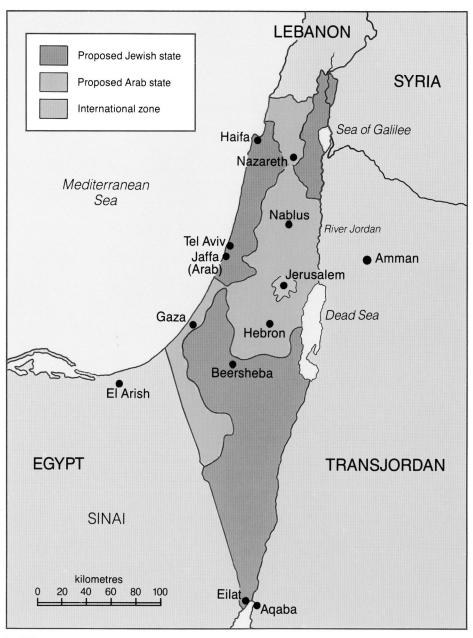

1: The UN partition plan, 1947

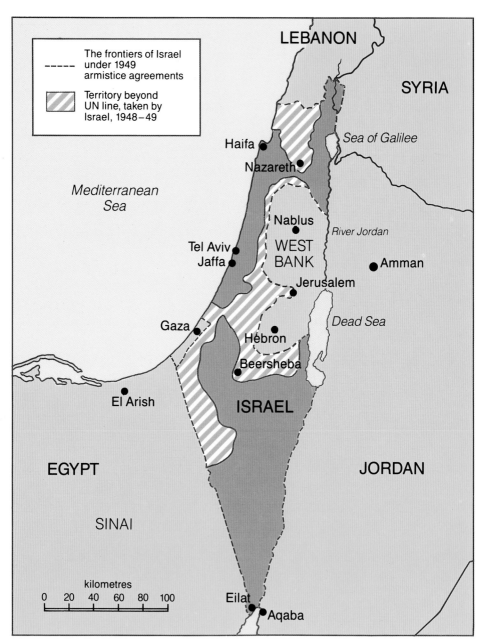

The frontiers of Israel under 1949 armistice agreements

Territory beyond UN line, taken by Israel, 1948–49

LEBANON

SYRIA

Mediterranean Sea

Haifa

Sea of Galilee

Nazareth

Nablus

River Jordan

Tel Aviv

WEST BANK

Jaffa

Amman

Jerusalem

Gaza

Dead Sea

Hebron

Beersheba

ISRAEL

El Arish

EGYPT

JORDAN

SINAI

kilometres

0   20   40   60   80   100

Eilat

Aqaba

2: Armistice boundaries, 1949

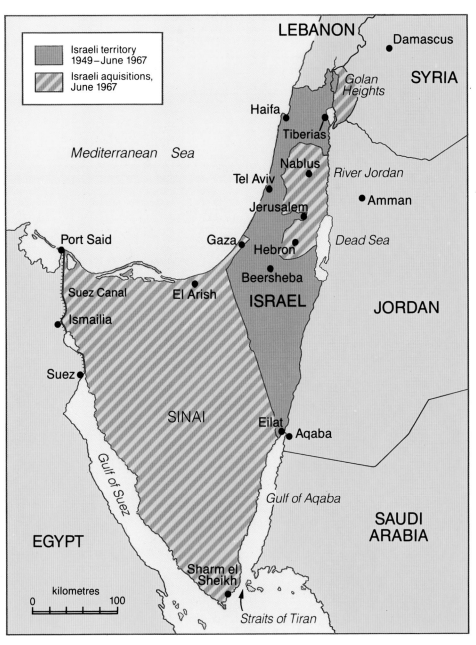

Legend:
- Israeli territory 1949–June 1967
- Israeli aquisitions, June 1967

LEBANON

Damascus

SYRIA

Golan Heights

Haifa

Tiberias

Mediterranean Sea

Nablus

River Jordan

Tel Aviv

Amman

Jerusalem

Port Said

Gaza

Hebron

Dead Sea

Suez Canal

El Arish

Beersheba

Ismailia

ISRAEL

JORDAN

Suez

SINAI

Eilat

Aqaba

Gulf of Suez

Gulf of Aqaba

EGYPT

SAUDI ARABIA

Sharm el Sheikh

kilometres

0   100

Straits of Tiran

3: 1967 Arab-Israeli War

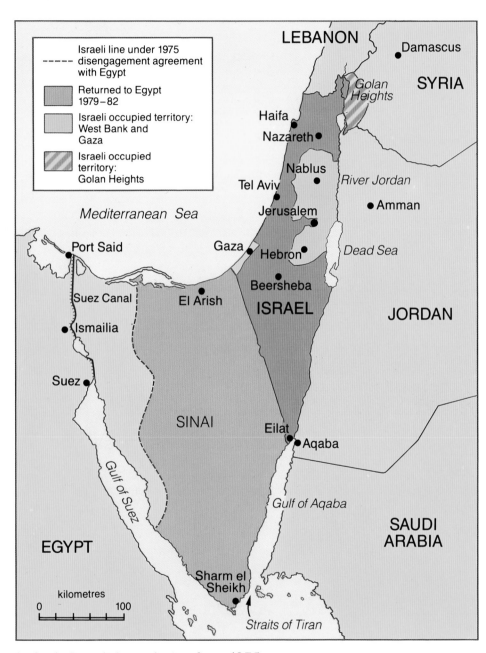

4: Arab-Israeli boundaries from 1975

Likud rejected any territorial compromise and urged continuing Jewish settlement throughout the West Bank and Gaza.

As a result, any prospect of greater Israeli flexibility did not materialise. *Likud* blocked Labour proposals for peace talks with the Arabs through a broader international conference rather than through the Camp David formula. The politically immobile national unity government represented the even balance between the major political party groups in Israel.

Palestinians and the *Intifada*

Outbreak of the *Intifada*

On 8 December 1987 four Palestinians were killed in a traffic accident in Gaza involving an Israeli vehicle. This incident provided the spark for the Palestinian popular uprising in the occupied territories—the *intifada*—which has since been maintained with varying degrees of intensity.

Israeli forces tried initially to contain the protests and demonstrations through repression, responding to stone-throwing Palestinian youths with live ammunition. The Israelis also resorted to the demolition of Palestinian houses, deportations, imprisonment without trial and beatings, the televised reporting of which greatly damaged Israel's reputation among friendly countries and Jewish communities abroad.

British Attitude

Britain voted in favour of two UN Security Council resolutions, adopted on 22 December 1987 and 5 January 1988, which condemned Israel's repressive practices and its deportation of Palestinian civilians. Such measures were in contravention of the Fourth Geneva Convention of 1949, which sets safeguards for people living under occupation and outlaws deportation.

Britain's views were also made known to the Israeli Government by the Foreign and Commonwealth Minister, David Mellor, during an official visit to Israel in early January 1988. Mr

Mellor criticised conditions in a Palestinian refugee camp in Gaza, pointing out that nothing had been done to improve the lot of the people during 20 years of Israeli administration. The Israeli authorities treated the occupation as an entirely military matter.

Mr Mellor did not accept the Israeli Government's assertion that the *intifada* was instigated by the Palestine Liberation Organisation or by Islamic fundamentalists. He believed that it was caused by genuine, broad-based and deep-seated Palestinian resentment at conditions in the occupied territories. Criticising the excessive force used by the Israeli authorities in dealing with the disturbances, he said that the problem could not be regarded as a short-term question of crowd control.

There could be no long-term peace and security in Israel until its occupation of Gaza and the West Bank was brought to an end and the Palestinians were given their right to self-determination. At the same time Mr Mellor emphasised that neighbouring states had to recognise Israel's right to exist behind secure boundaries.

In a further statement on 11 January 1988 Mr Mellor said that there was particular responsibility on the PLO to accept UN Security Council Resolutions 242 and 338 and to renounce violence. The organisation would not, he stressed, be brought into the framework unless it was prepared to do so. Britain had already cancelled high-level talks with a Jordanian–Palestinian delegation in 1985 because one of the Palestinian representatives would not accept these preconditions.

Jordanian Disengagement from the West Bank

A summit meeting of Arab League states was held in June 1988 to consider the Palestinian issue. It rejected a United States initiative which had been issued earlier in the year by the Secretary of State,

George Shultz, and demanded PLO participation in an international conference on an equal footing with the other parties.

In his address to the summit, King Hussein of Jordan expressed disillusionment with United States policy towards the Middle East. He endorsed the PLO as the sole representative of the Palestinian people and disclaimed any ambition to restore Jordanian rule in the Israeli-occupied West Bank.

The King's speech foreshadowed Jordan's formal disengagement from the West Bank at the end of July 1988, when legal and administrative links were severed. Henceforth Jordan would respect the wish of the Palestinians in the occupied territories to establish their own independent state in the West Bank.

Palestinian Declarations

In mid-November 1988 the Palestine National Council (PNC), meeting in Algiers, declared the occupied territories of West Bank and Gaza to be an independent Palestinian state. At the same time it accepted UN Security Council Resolution 242 of 1967 as the basis, together with the Palestinian right of self-determination, of an international peace conference. The Council also accepted Resolution 338 of 1973.

Further statements by Yasser Arafat in December 1988 reaffirmed the PNC's decisions, with more explicit recognition of the State of Israel and renunciation of all forms of terrorism.

On 15 December the UN General Assembly voted in favour of setting up an international conference on the Middle East under United Nations auspices with the participation of all parties on an equal footing, including the PLO. In another resolution the General Assembly acknowledged the PNC's declaration of a

Palestinian state. Britain and the other EC member states voted in favour of the first resolution and abstained from voting on the second, believing the PNC's declaration to be premature.

The Israeli Government indicated that it would consider peace talks with Arab states under United Nations or superpower auspices, but it would not talk to the PLO.

British Response

Britain and its European Community partners welcomed the positive Palestinian statements, as did the United States which lifted its ban on direct contacts with the PLO.

Foreign and Commonwealth Secretary Sir Geoffrey Howe made clear on 4 January 1989 that, while Britain respected Israel's wish to live peacefully within secure borders, this could not be achieved on the basis of the status quo. He said that it was time for Israel to acknowledge that a significant and positive move had been made by the Palestinians that required a constructive response.

Sir Geoffrey considered that it was vital for the Palestinians to continue to demonstrate their commitment to peace. The Israelis, for their part, had to be ready to explore Palestinian intentions rather than denounce them and to demonstrate their own good faith by reaffirming acceptance of UN Security Council Resolution 242 and the principle of exchanging territory for peace.

Following talks with Yasser Arafat in Tunis in mid-January 1989, the Foreign and Commonwealth Minister, William Waldegrave, said that the Palestinians, backed by the great majority of Arab states, had shifted to a more moderate stance. He added that the uprising in the occupied territories which had begun at the end of 1987 had produced a degree of solidarity among ordinary Palestinians that the Israelis could not ignore.

Diplomatic Stalemate, 1989–90

During 1989 diplomatic pressure for an international conference to resolve the Arab–Israeli conflict continued. In February the Soviet Foreign Minister toured the Middle East, advocating 'new thinking' on a peace settlement and proposing various ideas to encourage Israel to accept such a conference. The United States Government maintained its rejection of an international conference on terms envisaged by other parties, but made it clear that fresh thinking was expected from Israel.

Israeli Proposals

In April 1989 Prime Minister Shamir of Israel—whose right-wing *Likud* party was confirmed as the senior party in the new national unity coalition government following elections in late 1988—set out his own peace plan. It envisaged elections of local Palestinian representatives (excluding the PLO) who would negotiate with Israel on a transitional period of self-administration in the occupied territories, to be followed by negotiations on final status.

Reflecting the fragility of the national unity coalition, hardline members of *Likud* criticised the plan for conceding too much to the Palestinians while the Labour Party considered the plan too restrictive.

The PLO leader, Yasser Arafat, rejected Mr Shamir's proposals but backed the holding of elections in the West Bank and Gaza under international supervision following an Israeli military withdrawal. Other Arab reactions to the Israeli plan were generally dismissive.

The United States regarded the Israeli proposal for Palestinian elections as a positive step towards workable negotiations between the parties.

European Community Position
In June 1989, at the European Council meeting in Madrid, Britain and its partners reaffirmed the Community's policy defined in the Venice Declaration of 1980 and the statement of February 1987 (see p. 46). Reiterating its call for an international peace conference under the auspices of the United Nations as the appropriate forum for direct negotiations between the parties concerned, the Council broke new ground by adding that the PLO should participate in the process.

The Council welcomed the support given by the Arab League, at a summit meeting in May 1989, to the decision by the Palestine National Council to renounce terrorism and recognise Israel's right to exist. It also applauded efforts undertaken by the United States in its contacts with the parties directly concerned, and particularly the dialogue entered into with the PLO.

The Council deplored the continuing violence and casualties in the occupied territories, engendered by the Palestinian *intifada* and Israeli repression. Regarding the proposals put forward by Mr Shamir, it welcomed elections in the occupied territories provided that:

— they were set in the context of a process towards a comprehensive, just and lasting settlement of the conflict;

— they took place in the occupied territories, including East Jerusalem, 'under adequate guarantees of freedom'; and

— no solution was excluded, and the final negotiation took place on the basis of UN Security Council Resolutions 242 and 338.

Deadlock

Little diplomatic progress ensued from the Shamir plan, partly because of the differences within the Israeli national unity coalition over the scope of the initiative and the nature of Palestinian representation.

Against the background of the continuing Palestinian *intifada*, attempts were made during the rest of 1989 by Egypt (now reintegrated into the Arab fold) and by the United States to clarify the Israeli Government's position and to advance the process of negotiation.

At the same time, the mass immigration of Soviet Jews to Israel added a further complicating factor. Prime Minister Shamir's statement in January 1990 that Israel must keep the occupied territories to accommodate the immigrants provoked alarm among Arab states and disapproval by the United States.

Failure to reach a workable consensus within the Israeli coalition led ultimately to its collapse in March 1990. In June 1990 Mr Shamir formed a coalition of right-wing parties headed by *Likud*, thereby reducing still further the prospects of an Israeli dialogue with the Palestinians. The United States expressed concern over the attitude of the Israeli Government, at the same time suspending its dialogue with the PLO in response to acts of terrorism by Palestinian extremists.

British Statement

Citing the pace of political change in Eastern Europe and South Africa, the Foreign and Commonwealth Secretary, Douglas Hurd, said in a speech in May 1990 that he did not believe that the prospects for a settlement in the Middle East were hopeless. He stressed, however, that the 'moving force for change cannot be vio-lence because violence in fact begets only violence'.

The Jordanian disengagement of 1988, by which Jordan relin-quished administrative and judicial responsibility for the West Bank, had opened the way, said Mr Hurd, for the commitments given by the Palestine National Council and the PLO to recognise the existence of Israel and to renounce terrorism (see p. 50). The onus was on Israel to enter into a dialogue with representative Palestinians. The key to a settlement had to be an exchange of ter-ritory for peace.

Mr Hurd acknowledged Arab concern over the issue of immi-gration of Soviet Jews into Israel. Although Britain did not oppose Jewish immigration, any such settlement in the occupied territories of Gaza, the West Bank, the Golan Heights or East Jerusalem was 'contrary to international law, needlessly provocative and an enor-mous complication in the search for a negotiated settlement'. It was in these territories, he said, that Palestinians had eventually to be free to exercise their right to self-determination.

In addition to the essential component of direct Israeli–Palestinian negotiation, Britain continued to favour an international peace conference on the Middle East. It was necessary to establish the legal framework of an agreement between the par-ties because an eventual structure of peace would need underpin-ning by the international community if it was going to remain stable.

Mr Hurd warned that it would be dangerous to move back to a stage where there was no peace process, and that a collapse of negotiations would not suit Israeli interests. He said that the 'men of violence, wherever they may be, would then feel justified in turning on the PLO, turning on other Arab leaders, arguing that their reasonableness has been in vain and that the terrorist war, even if it took many years, was the only answer for the Palestinians'.

The Gulf Crisis

Iraq's aggression against its small neighbour, Kuwait, in August 1990,[13] creating an international crisis, proved to have a significant effect on the development of the Arab–Israeli conflict.

Iraq's invasion and military occupation of Kuwait, in defiance of a series of UN Security Council resolutions, provoked not only condemnation but also unprecedented co-operation in the international community to reverse the aggression. A multinational military force—Britain's contribution to which was the largest of any European country—was assembled in the Gulf region during the months after August 1990.

When it became clear that Iraq would respond neither to the UN Security Council resolutions nor to other diplomatic initiatives, armed force was initiated by the international coalition in mid-January 1991. Following a brief and successful campaign, the coalition effected an Iraqi withdrawal from Kuwait and hostilities were suspended at the end of February.

Palestinian Support for Iraq

Soon after the invasion, President Saddam Hussein of Iraq sought to deflect criticism of his actions by trying to link an Iraqi withdrawal from Kuwait to an Israeli withdrawal from the occupied territories. As a consequence most Palestinians, and some other Arab popular opinion, backed Iraq against the international coalition.

---

[13] For more information see *Britain and the Gulf Crisis* (Aspects of Britain: HMSO, 1993).

British View

Britain dismissed Iraq's claim to be championing the Palestinian cause and suspended ministerial contacts with the PLO because of Yasser Arafat's support for Saddam Hussein. On 4 October 1990 Mr Hurd criticised the PLO for having 'found excuses for the occupation of an Arab land' by Iraq. The organisation, he warned, had put at risk the progress it had made in gaining international respect and had weakened the Palestinian cause.

He added: 'With Iraq out of Kuwait, it is moderate Arab opinion which will triumph and will be in the ascendancy over the extremists. This should be an opportunity ... [to] ... bring about at last the chance to secure acceptance of the State of Israel behind secure borders.'

The United States Government similarly indicated that the resolution of the Gulf crisis could be a 'springboard' for the settlement of the Arab–Israeli conflict.

Killings in Jerusalem, October 1990

The diversion of international attention from the Arab–Israeli dispute by Iraq's occupation of Kuwait was interrupted on 8 October when Israeli security forces in Jerusalem shot dead some 20 Palestinians. This followed violence involving Palestinians and Jewish worshippers around Temple Mount, a site sacred to both Muslims and Jews. More than 150 people were injured. Further clashes between Israeli troops and Palestinian demonstrators occurred on 10 October.

The UN Security Council condemned the Israeli actions in a resolution, 672 (1990), unanimously adopted on 13 October. It reaffirmed that a lasting solution to the Arab–Israeli conflict had to take into account the right to security for all states in the region, including Israel, as well as the legitimate rights of the Palestinian people. Resolution 672 condemned the 'acts of violence committed by the Israeli security forces resulting in injuries and loss of human life' on 8 October and called on Israel to abide by its legal obligations and responsibilities in the occupied territories under the Fourth Geneva Convention.

Western leaders, together with their Arab allies, were concerned that the Jerusalem killings should not provide an opportunity for Saddam Hussein to exploit, capitalising on Palestinian sympathy for Iraq in the Gulf crisis. They continued to deny any linkage between Iraqi aggression against Kuwait and the Arab–Israeli dispute.

Speaking in Egypt on 14 October, Mr Hurd repeated Britain's condemnation of Israel's 'excessive use of force' against the Palestinians in Jerusalem. He added that the 'international community, including Israel's closest friends, feel anxiety and more at Israel's actions'.

An official British statement on 17 October reiterated British policy on a Palestinian state—Britain favoured self-determination for the Palestinian people: whether or not that led to a state was a matter for them and for negotiation.

Israel and the Gulf War

Military action by the international coalition to expel Iraq from Kuwait commenced in mid-January 1991. Reflecting popular sympathy for Iraq in Jordan, King Hussein contrasted this with the lack of action to implement UN resolutions calling for Israeli withdrawal from the occupied territories.

Iraq carried out its threats to attack Israel from the outset of hostilities with the international coalition. About 40 Iraqi Scud missiles were fired into Israel before the ceasefire at the end of February 1991. These caused some material damage but relatively few casualties. Britain and its coalition partners applauded Israel's restraint in the face of the unprovoked Iraqi attacks.

Middle East Peace Process

The Foreign and Commonwealth Secretary said on 26 February 1991 that although Saddam Hussein had set back the Palestinian cause, abetted by the mistakes of the PLO leadership, there would have to be a return to the issue after Iraq's defeat. Earlier on 19 February, the European Community stated that the Arab–Israeli dispute was a fundamental cause of regional instability and that without a solution there could be no lasting peace.

United States Initiative

At the end of the Gulf conflict, the United States Secretary of State, James Baker, embarked on a series of visits to the Middle East aiming to secure acceptance of an initiative for a peace conference. The core of the US proposals included the following elements:

— co-sponsorship by the United States and the then Soviet Union, participation by the European Community Presidency and observer status for the United Nations;

— simultaneous direct discussions, under the umbrella of the conference, between Israel and its Arab neighbours and between Israel and the Palestinians;

— negotiations on the basis of UN Security Council Resolutions 242 and 338;

— no preconditions on the nature of an eventual settlement, precluding, for example, any commitment on a separate Palestinian state; and

—representation of the Palestinians by figures from outside the PLO, probably in a joint delegation with Jordan.

Diplomatic Progress

Responses by Arab states to the United States initiative were positive. The Syrian Government accepted the proposals unconditionally on 14 July. On 19 July 1991 President Mubarak of Egypt said that, if Israel stopped building settlements in the occupied territories, he thought that Arab states would end their boycott of Israel. Such a proposal, endorsed by Saudi Arabia, was put forward by the leaders of the seven major industrialised nations, including Britain, at their London summit meeting from 15 to 17 July. At the same time, the Jordanian Prime Minister issued an invitation to Palestinians to come to Amman to discuss the idea of a joint Jordanian–Palestinian delegation.

On 29 July European Community member states declared that they would make 'their full contribution as a participant' in the peace process.

At their summit meeting in Moscow at the end of July 1991, the United States President, George Bush, and the Soviet President, Mikhail Gorbachev, issued a joint declaration on the Middle East pledging to promote and sustain the peacemaking process. Both countries, acting as co-sponsors, would work to convene in October 1991 a peace conference designed to launch bilateral and multilateral negotiations.

Under pressure to respond flexibly, Israel expressed its willingness in early August to enter peace negotiations in accordance with the United States initiative, 'subject to a satisfactory solution of the issue of Palestinian Arab representation in the Jordanian–Palestinian delegation'. Israel opposed the inclusion in any such delegation of recognised members of the PLO or any Palestinians from East Jerusalem. The Israeli Government agreed in June to the participation in any conference of the European Community Presidency 'alongside the United States and the USSR'.

British View

Britain supported the United States initiative from its outset and urged all parties concerned to show flexibility. On 5 August a Foreign and Commonwealth Office spokesman said that Britain hoped that agreement could be reached in a way which made the Palestinian delegation representative and enabled the peace conference to start. He added that Britain had always regarded East Jerusalem as part of the occupied territories rather than part of the capital of Israel.

Peace Process, October 1991 to mid-December 1992

The peace conference was inaugurated on 30 October 1991. In addition to United States, Soviet and European Community representation, the opening stages (held in Madrid) were attended by delegations from Israel, Syria, Egypt and Lebanon and by a joint Jordanian–Palestinian delegation.

Commenting in November on these developments, Foreign and Commonwealth Minister Douglas Hogg said that nobody expected 'instant, spectacular results'. However, he continued: 'At Madrid history was made in that for the first time representative Israelis and Palestinians sat together, at least implicitly acknowledging each other's independent status and that the solution to their bitter dispute lay in negotiation rather than conflict.'

Over the course of the following year several further rounds of negotiations were held. The process moved slowly and with little progress on substance. At the same time the negative cycle of violence in the region continued, revolving around the *intifada*, Palestinian attacks on Israeli targets and Israeli military retaliation.

However, in a speech on 23 November 1992, the Foreign and Commonwealth Secretary, Mr Hurd, summarised Britain's optimism: 'Looking back it would have been inconceivable, even perhaps 18 months ago, that the progress should have been such that Arabs and Israelis are now deeply engaged in direct talks. The atmosphere at the various meetings shows that the attitudes have developed a good deal on all sides since the historic first meeting at Madrid. There is the slow but visible growth of new understandings.'

European Community Position

At the inaugural session of the conference the Community and its member states pledged their constructive partnership in all phases of the negotiations. Reaffirming this commitment in a declaration in December 1991, the European Council said that a halt to Israel's settlement activity in the occupied territories and a renunciation of the Arab trade boycott against Israel would help to create the stable environment which progress in the negotiations required.

In a further statement in June 1992 the European Council expressed its belief that the results of the election in Israel earlier in the month—in which *Likud* was defeated and the Labour Party regained power—would reinforce the peace process and the commitment to a lasting settlement. It hoped that the new Israeli

Government and the Arab parties would act quickly to implement confidence-building measures.

On 12 December 1992 the Council, meeting in Edinburgh, reiterated its full support for the peace process in both its bilateral and multilateral aspects, and the role of Russia and the United States as co-sponsors. The peace process represented an opportunity which had to be seized if dangers to the stability of the Middle East region were to be avoided.

Deportation of Palestinians

On 16 December 1992 Israel deported more than 400 Palestinians over the border with Lebanon. This action represented a crackdown on Islamic fundamentalist groups following attacks on Israeli soldiers in the occupied territories and the murder of a border guard, kidnapped within Israel's pre-1967 borders. In response, Arab states warned that the expulsions could undermine the Middle East peace process.

The Lebanese Government refused to accept any responsibility for the Palestinian deportees, who were isolated in a makeshift camp in the north of the Israeli-imposed security zone in southern Lebanon. Israel similarly refused to readmit them. Efforts by a special United Nations representative, Mr James Jonah, who visited Israel and Lebanon in late December in a bid to arrange a compromise, proved fruitless.

British View

In its capacity as president of the European Community, Britain issued a statement on 17 December expressing concern about events in Israel and the occupied territories. It condemned the murder of the Israeli border guard and called on all parties 'to exercise restraint in order to ensure that extremists do not succeed in their objective of undermining the peace process'.

The statement urged the Israeli authorities not to pursue the policy of deportations, describing it as a violation of the Fourth Geneva Convention.

European Community Statement

In a further statement on 18 December, Britain and its EC partners expressed regret over the failure of the Israeli Government to respond to the appeal not to pursue the policy of deportations, adding that it infringed the sovereignty of Lebanon.

The statement continued: 'Recent events underline the fact that the peace process is the only way to resolve the problems of the region. The European Community and its member states call on all parties to redouble their efforts to negotiate a just, lasting and comprehensive settlement.'

UN Security Council Resolution

On 18 December the UN Security Council adopted unanimously Resolution 799 (1992). This strongly condemned the action taken by Israel, as the occupying power, to deport hundreds of Palestinian civilians. It reaffirmed the applicability of the Fourth Geneva Convention to all the Palestinian territories occupied by Israel since 1967, including Jerusalem. Resolution 799 maintained that deportation of civilians constituted a contravention of Israel's obligations under that Convention.

The Security Council reaffirmed the independence, sovereignty and territorial integrity of Lebanon, and demanded that Israel ensure the safe and immediate return to the occupied territories of all those deported. In addition, the Resolution requested the UN Secretary-General to consider despatching a representative to the area to liaise with the Israeli Government (see p. 65).

Developments from January to April 1993
A second UN envoy visited the region in early January but his mission achieved little more than Mr Jonah's. Also in January British helicopters provided support for an International Committee of the Red Cross humanitarian mission to the Palestinian deportees.

On 1 February 1993 the Israeli Government decided to allow 100 of the deportees to return and to halve the term of exile to one year for the remainder. This followed an earlier Israeli decision in mid-January to remove the legal bar against contacts with the Palestine Liberation Organisation.

The Foreign and Commonwealth Secretary, Mr Hurd, said on 10 February that the Israeli concession on the deportations was 'not sufficient, but it is a step in the right direction'. He also expressed satisfaction that the new United States Administration was giving the peace process a high priority.

On 9 March Douglas Hogg had a meeting with two PLO representatives and the head of the Palestinian negotiating team in the Middle East peace process. This meeting marked the resumption of British ministerial contacts with the PLO which had been suspended in 1990 as a result of the PLO's failure to condemn Iraq's invasion of Kuwait (see p. 57).

In the meeting, Mr Hogg stressed the importance of all sides resuming the peace talks. He acknowledged Palestinian concern over deportations by Israel and recognised that further Israeli movement on that question would facilitate a Palestinian return to the negotiating table.

Mr Hogg added: 'This is a very important moment. The present Israeli Prime Minister, Mr Rabin, is the Prime Minister most likely to be able to make a long-lasting agreement between the Palestinians and the Israelis. Therefore, this is not an opportunity to lose and that is why it was so important to persuade the Palestinians to go back into the talks.'

Mr Hurd similarly urged progress towards an early resumption of the peace process at a meeting on 11 March with the Israeli Deputy Foreign Minister, Yossi Beilin. Mr Beilin stressed the importance which Israel attached to participation by Britain and the European Community in the multilateral negotiations.

Peace talks attended by all the parties reconvened at the end of April.

Documentation

Most of the following extracts are abridged and headings have been added.

1: The Balfour Declaration

November 2nd, 1917

Balfour was British Foreign Secretary, Rothschild the British Zionist Leader.

Dear Lord Rothschild,

I have much pleasure in conveying to you on behalf of His Majesty's Government the following declaration of sympathy with Jewish Zionist aspirations, which has been submitted to and approved by the Cabinet.

'His Majesty's Government view with favour the establishment in Palestine of a national home for the Jewish people, and will use their best endeavours to facilitate the achievement of this object, it being clearly understood that nothing shall be done which may prejudice the civil and religious rights of existing non-Jewish communities in Palestine, or the rights and political status enjoyed by Jews in any other country.'

I should be grateful if you would bring this declaration to the knowledge of the Zionist Federation.

Yours sincerely,

Arthur James Balfour.

2: Extracts from The British Mandate

The Council of the League of Nations:

Whereas the Principal Allied Powers have agreed, for the purpose of giving effect to the provisions of Article 22 of the Covenant of the League of Nations, to entrust to a Mandatory selected by the said Powers the administration of the territory of Palestine, which formerly belonged to the Turkish Empire, within such boundaries as may be fixed by them; and

Whereas the Principal Allied Powers have also agreed that the Mandatory should be responsible for putting into effect the declaration originally made on 2 November 1917 by the Government of His Britannic Majesty, and adopted by the said Powers, in favour of the establishment in Palestine of a national home for the Jewish people, it being clearly understood that nothing should be done which might prejudice the civil and religious rights of existing non-Jewish communities in Palestine, or the rights and political status enjoyed by Jews in any other country; and

Whereas recognition has thereby been given to the historical connexion of the Jewish people with Palestine and to the grounds for reconstituting their national home in that country; and

Whereas the Principal Allied Powers have selected His Britannic Majesty as the Mandatory for Palestine; and

Whereas the mandate in respect of Palestine has been formulated in the following terms and submitted to the Council of the League for approval; and

Whereas His Britannic Majesty has accepted the mandate in respect of Palestine and undertaken to exercise it on behalf of the League of Nations in conformity with the following provisions; and

Whereas by the aforementioned Article 22 (paragraph 8), it is provided that the degree of authority, control or administration to be exercised by the Mandatory, not having been previously agreed upon by the Members of the League, shall be explicitly defined by the Council of the League of Nations;

Terms of the Mandate

Confirming the said Mandate, defines its terms as follows:

ARTICLE 1

The Mandatory shall have full powers of legislation and of administration, save as they may be limited by the terms of this mandate.

ARTICLE 2

The Mandatory shall be responsible for placing the country under such political, administrative and economic conditions as will secure the establishment of the Jewish national home, as laid down in the preamble, and the development of self-governing institutions, and also for safeguarding the civil and religious rights of all the inhabitants of Palestine irrespective of race and religion.

ARTICLE 3

The Mandatory shall, so far as circumstances permit, encourage local autonomy.

ARTICLE 4

An appropriate Jewish agency shall be recognized as a public body for the purpose of advising and co-operating with the Administration of Palestine in such economic, social and other matters as may affect the establishment of the Jewish national home and the interests of the Jewish population in Palestine, and, subject always to the control of the Administration, to assist and take part in the development of the country.

The Zionist Organization, so long as its organization and constitution are in the opinion of the Mandatory appropriate, shall be recognized as such agency. It shall take steps in consultation with His Britannic Majesty's Government to secure the co-operation of all Jews who are willing to assist in the establishment of the Jewish national home.

ARTICLE 5

The Mandatory shall be responsible for seeing that no Palestine territory shall be ceded or leased to, or in any way placed under the control of, the Government of any foreign Power.

ARTICLE 6

The Administration of Palestine, while ensuring that the rights and position of other sections of the population are not prejudiced, shall facilitate Jewish immigration under suitable conditions and shall encourage, in co-operation with the Jewish agency referred to in Article 4, close settlement by Jews on the land, including State lands and waste lands not required for public purposes.

ARTICLE 7

The Administration of Palestine shall be responsible for enacting a nationality law. There shall be included in this law provisions framed so as to facilitate the acquisition of Palestinian citizenship by Jews who take up their permanent residence in Palestine...

Holy Places

ARTICLE 13

All responsibility in connexion with the Holy Places and religious buildings or sites in Palestine, including that of preserving existing rights and of securing free access to the Holy Places, religious buildings and sites and the free exercise of worship, while ensuring the requirements of public order and decorum, is assumed by the Mandatory, who shall be responsible solely to the League of Nations in all matters connected herewith, provided that nothing in this article shall prevent the Mandatory from entering into such arrangements as he may deem reasonable with the Administration for the purpose of carrying the provisions of this article into effect; and provided also that nothing in this Mandate shall be construed as conferring upon the Mandatory authority to interfere with the fabric or the management of purely Muslim sacred shrines, the immunities of which are guaranteed.

ARTICLE 14

A special Commission shall be appointed by the Mandatory to study, define and determine the rights and claims in connexion with the Holy Places and the rights and claims relating to the different religious communities in Palestine. The method of nomination, the composition and the functions of this Commission shall be submitted to the Council of the League for its approval, and the Commission shall not be appointed or enter upon its functions without the approval of the Council.

Human Rights

ARTICLE 15

The Mandatory shall see that complete freedom of conscience and the free exercise of all forms of worship, subject only to the maintenance of public order and morals, are ensured to all. No discrimination of any kind shall be made between the inhabitants of Palestine on the ground of race, religion or language. No person shall be excluded from Palestine on the sole ground of his religious belief.

The right of each community to maintain its own schools for the education of its own members in its own language, while conforming to such educational requirements of a general nature as the Administration may impose, shall not be denied or impaired...

ARTICLE 22

English, Arabic and Hebrew shall be the official languages of Palestine. Any statement or inscription in Arabic on stamps or money in Palestine shall be repeated in Hebrew and any statement or inscription in Hebrew shall be repeated in Arabic...

ARTICLE 24

The Mandatory shall make to the Council of the League of Nations an annual report to the satisfaction of the Council as to the measures taken during the year to carry out the provisions of the mandate. Copies of all laws and regulations promulgated or issued during the year shall be communicated with the report...

ARTICLE 28

In the event of the termination of the mandate hereby conferred upon the Mandatory, the Council of the League of Nations shall make such arrangements as may be deemed necessary for safeguarding in perpetuity, under guarantee of the League, the rights secured by Articles 13 and 14, and shall use its influence for securing, under the guarantee of the League, that the Government of Palestine will fully honour the financial obligations legitimately incurred by the Administration of Palestine during the period of the mandate, including the rights of public servants to pensions or gratuities.

The present instrument shall be deposited in original in the archives of the League of Nations and certified copies shall be forwarded by the Secretary General of the League of Nations to all Members of the League.

3: The Churchill Memorandum

Extract from the statement of British policy in Palestine issued by Mr Winston Churchill in June 1922.

The Secretary of State for the Colonies has given renewed consideration to the existing political situation in Palestine, with a very earnest desire to arrive at a settlement of the outstanding questions which have given rise to uncertainty and unrest among certain sections of the population. After consultation with the High Commissioner for Palestine the following statement has been drawn up. It summarizes the essential parts of the correspondence that has already taken place between the Secretary of State and a Delegation from the Muslim Christian Society of Palestine, which has been for some time in England, and it states the further conclusions which have since been reached.

Arabs and Jews

The tension which has prevailed from time to time in Palestine is mainly due to apprehensions, which are entertained both by sections of the Arab and by sections of the Jewish population. These apprehensions, so far as the Arabs are concerned, are partly based upon exaggerated interpretations of the meaning of the Declaration favouring the establishment of a Jewish National Home in Palestine, made on behalf of His Majesty's Government on 2 November 1917. Unauthorized statements have been made to the effect that the purpose in view is to create a wholly Jewish Palestine. Phrases have been used such as that Palestine is to become 'as Jewish as England is English'. His Majesty's Government regard any such expectation as impracticable and have no such aim in view. Nor have they at any time contemplated, as appears to be feared by the Arab Delegation, the disappearance or the subordination of the Arabic population, language, or culture in Palestine. They would draw attention to the fact that the terms of the Declaration referred to do not contemplate that Palestine as a whole should be converted into a Jewish National Home, but that such a Home should be founded *in Palestine*. In this connexion it has been observed with satisfaction that at the meeting of the Zionist Congress, the supreme governing body of the Zionist Organization, held at Carlsbad in September 1921, a resolution was passed expressing as the official statement of Zionist aims 'the determination of the Jewish people to live with the Arab people on terms of unity and mutual respect, and together with them to make the common home into a flourishing community, the upbuilding of which may assure to each of its peoples an undisturbed national development'.

It is also necessary to point out that the Zionist Commission in Palestine, now termed the Palestine Zionist Executive, has not desired to possess, and does not possess, any share in the general administration of the country. Nor does the special position assigned to the Zionist Organization in Article 4 of the Draft Mandate for Palestine imply any such functions. That special position relates to the measures to be taken in Palestine affecting the Jewish population, and contemplates that the Organization may assist in the general development of the country, but does not entitle it to share in any degree in its Government.

Further, it is contemplated that the status of all citizens of Palestine in the eyes of the law shall be Palestinian, and it has never been intended that they, or any section of them, should possess any other juridical status.

So far as the Jewish population of Palestine are concerned it appears that some among them are apprehensive that His Majesty's Government may depart from the policy embodied in the Declaration of 1917. It is necessary, therefore, once more to affirm that these fears are unfounded, and that that Declaration, re-affirmed by the Conference of the Principal Allied Powers at San Remo and again in the Treaty of Sèvres, is not susceptible of change.

The Jewish Community

During the last two or three generations the Jews have recreated in Palestine a community, now numbering 80,000, of whom about one fourth are farmers or workers upon the land. This community has its own political organs; an elected assembly for the direction of its domestic concerns; elected councils in the towns; and an organization for the control of its schools. It has its elected Chief Rabbinate and Rabbinical Council for the direction of its religious affairs. Its business is conducted in Hebrew as a vernacular language, and a Hebrew press serves its needs. It has its distinctive intellectual life and displays considerable economic activity. This community, then, with its town and country population, its political, religious, and social organizations, its own language, its own customs, its own life, has in fact 'national' characteristics. When it is asked what is meant by the development of the Jewish National Home in Palestine it may be answered that it is not the imposition of a Jewish nationality upon the inhabitants of Palestine as a whole, but the further development of the existing Jewish community, with the assistance of Jews in other parts of the world, in order that it may become a centre in which the Jewish people as a whole may take, on grounds of religion and race, an interest and a pride. But in order that this community should have the best prospect of free development and provide a full opportunity for the Jewish people to display its capacities, it is essential that it should know that it is in Palestine as of right and not on sufferance. That is the reason why it is necessary that the existence of a Jewish National Home in Palestine should be internationally guaranteed, and that it should be formally recognized to rest upon ancient historic connexion.

This, then, is the interpretation which His Majesty's Government place upon the Declaration of 1917, and, so understood, the Secretary of State is of the opinion that it does not contain or imply anything which need cause either alarm to the Arab population of Palestine or disappointment to the Jews.

For the fulfilment of this policy it is necessary that the Jewish community in Palestine should be able to increase its numbers by immigration. This immigration cannot be so great in volume as to exceed whatever may be the economic capacity of the country at the time to absorb new arrivals. It is essential to ensure that the immigrants should not be a burden upon the people of Palestine as a whole, and that they should not deprive any section of the present population of their employment. Hitherto the immigration has fulfilled these conditions. The number of immigrants since the British occupation has been about 25,000...

4: Extracts from the Peel Commission Report (July 1937)

Having reached the conclusion that there is no possibility of solving the Palestine problem under the existing Mandate (or even under a scheme of cantonization), the Commission recommend the termination of the present Mandate on the basis of Partition and put forward a definite scheme which they consider to be practicable, honourable and just. The scheme is as follows:

The Mandate for Palestine should terminate and be replaced by a Treaty System in accordance with the precedent set in Iraq and Syria.

Two States

Under Treaties to be negotiated by the Mandatory with the Government of Transjordan and representatives of the Arabs of Palestine on the one hand, and with the Zionist Organization on the other, it would be declared that two sovereign independent States would shortly be established—(1) an Arab State consisting of Transjordan united with that part of Palestine allotted to the Arabs, (2) a Jewish State consisting of that part of Palestine allotted to the Jews. The Mandatory would undertake to support any requests for admission to the League of Nations made by the Governments of the Arab and Jewish States. The Treaties would include strict guarantees for the protection of minorities. Military Conventions would be attached to the Treaties.

A new Mandate should be instituted to execute the trust of maintaining the sanctity of Jerusalem and Bethlehem and ensuring free and safe access to them for all the world. An enclave should be demarcated to which this Mandate should apply, extending from a point north of Jerusalem to a point south of Bethlehem, and access to the sea should be provided by a corridor extending from Jerusalem to Jaffa. The policy of the Balfour Declaration would not apply to the Mandated Area.

The Jewish State should pay a subvention to the Arab State. A Finance Commission should be appointed to advise as to its amount and as to the division of the public debt of Palestine and other financial questions.

5: Extracts from the White Paper of 1939

... 4. It has been urged that the expression 'a national home for the Jewish people' offered a prospect that Palestine might in due course become a Jewish State or Commonwealth. His Majesty's Government do not wish to contest the view, which was expressed by the Royal Commission, that the Zionist leaders at the time of the issue of the Balfour Declaration recognized that an ultimate Jewish State was not precluded by the terms of the Declaration. But, with the Royal Commission, His Majesty's Government believe that the framers of the Mandate in which the Balfour Declaration was embodied could not have intended that Palestine should be converted into a Jewish State against the will of the Arab population of the country ...

His Majesty's Government therefore now declare unequivocally that it is not part of their policy that Palestine should become a Jewish State. They would indeed regard it as contrary to their obligations to the Arabs under the Mandate, as well as to the assurances which have been given to the Arab people in the past, that the Arab population of Palestine should be made the subjects of a Jewish State against their will ...

10. ... His Majesty's Government make the following declaration of their intentions regarding the future government of Palestine:

Palestine State

(i) The objective of His Majesty's Government is the establishment within ten years of an independent Palestine State in such treaty relations with the United Kingdom as will provide satisfactorily for the commercial and strategic requirements of both countries in the future. This proposal for the establishment of the independent State would involve consultation with the Council of the League of Nations with a view to the termination of the Mandate.

(ii) The independent State should be one in which Arabs and Jews share in government in such a way as to ensure that the essential interests of each community are safeguarded.

Transitional Period

(iii) The establishment of the independent State will be preceded by a transitional period throughout which His Majesty's Government will retain responsibility for the government of the country. During the transitional period the people of Palestine will be given an increasing part in the government of their country. Both sections of the population will have an opportunity to participate in the machinery of government, and the process will be carried on whether or not they both avail themselves of it.

(iv) As soon as peace and order have been sufficiently restored in Palestine steps will be taken to carry out this policy of giving the people of Palestine an increasing part in the government of their country, the objective being to place Palestinians in charge of all the Departments of Government, with the assistance of British advisers and subject to the control of the High Commissioner. With this object in view His Majesty's Government will be prepared immediately to arrange that Palestinians shall be placed in charge of certain Departments, with British advisers. The Palestinian heads of Departments will sit on the Executive Council, which advises the High Commissioner. Arab and Jewish representatives will be invited to serve as heads of Departments approximately in proportion to their respective populations. The number of Palestinians in charge of Departments will be increased as circumstances permit until all heads of Departments are Palestinians, exercising the administrative and advisory functions which are at present performed by British officials. When that stage is reached consideration will be given to the question of converting the Executive Council into a Council of Ministers with a consequential change in the status and functions of the Palestinian heads of Departments.

(v) His Majesty's Government make no proposals at this stage regarding the establishment of an elective legislature. Nevertheless they would regard this as an appropriate constitutional development, and should public opinion in Palestine hereafter show itself in favour of such a development, they will be prepared, provided that local conditions permit, to establish the necessary machinery.

Review of Constitutional Arrangements

(vi) At the end of five years from the restoration of peace and order, an appropriate body representative of the people of Palestine and of His Majesty's Government will be set up to review the working of the constitutional arrangements during the transitional period and to consider and make recommendations regarding the Constitution of the independent Palestine State.

(vii) His Majesty's Government will require to be satisfied that in the treaty contemplated by sub-paragraph (i) or in the Constitution contemplated by sub-paragraph (vi) adequate provision has been made for:

(a) the security of, and freedom of access to, the Holy Places, and the protection of the interests and property of the various religious bodies;

(b) the protection of the different communities in Palestine in accordance with the obligations of His Majesty's Government to both Arabs and Jews and for the special position in Palestine of the Jewish National Home;

(c) such requirements to meet the strategic situation as may be regarded as necessary by His Majesty's Government in the light of the circumstances then existing.

His Majesty's Government will also require to be satisfied that the interests of certain foreign countries in Palestine, for the preservation of which they are at present responsible, are adequately safeguarded.

(viii) His Majesty's Government will do everything in their power to create conditions which will enable the independent Palestine State to come into
being within ten years. If, at the end of ten years, it appears to His
Majesty's Government that, contrary to their hope, circumstances require
the postponement of the establishment of the independent State, they will
consult with representatives of the people of Palestine, the Council of the
League of Nations and the neighbouring Arab States before deciding on
such a postponement. If His Majesty's Government come to the conclusion that postponement is unavoidable, they will invite the co-operation of
these parties in framing plans for the future with a view to achieving the
desired objective at the earliest possible date.

11. During the transitional period steps will be taken to increase the powers and
responsibilities of municipal corporations and local councils...

Immigration

14. . . . they believe that they will be acting consistently with their Mandatory obligations to both Arabs and Jews, and in the manner best calculated to serve the
interests of the whole people of Palestine by adopting the following proposals
regarding immigration:

(i) Jewish immigration during the next five years will be at a rate which, if
economic absorptive capacity permits, will bring the Jewish population up
to approximately one-third of the total population of the country. Taking
into account the expected natural increase of the Arab and Jewish populations, and the number of illegal Jewish immigrants now in the country, this
would allow of the admission, as from the beginning of April this year, of
some 75,000 immigrants over the next five years. These immigrants
would, subject to the criterion of economic absorptive capacity, be admitted as follows:

(a) For each of the next five years a quota of 10,000 Jewish immigrants
will be allowed, on the understanding that a shortage in any one year
may be added to the quotas for subsequent years, within the five-year
period, if economic absorptive capacity permits.

(b) In addition, as a contribution towards the solution of the Jewish
refugee problem, 25,000 refugees will be admitted as soon as the High

Commissioner is satisfied that adequate provision for their maintenance is ensured, special consideration being given to refugee children and dependants.

(ii) The existing machinery for ascertaining economic absorptive capacity will be retained, and the High Commissioner will have the ultimate responsibility for deciding the limits of economic capacity. Before each periodic decision is taken, Jewish and Arab representatives will be consulted.

(iii) After the period of five years no further Jewish immigration will be permitted unless the Arabs of Palestine are prepared to acquiesce in it.

(iv) His Majesty's Government are determined to check illegal immigration, and further preventive measures are being adopted. The numbers of any Jewish illegal immigrants who, despite these measures, may succeed in coming into the country and cannot be deported will be deducted from the yearly quotas.

15. His Majesty's Government are satisfied that, when the immigration over five years which is now contemplated has taken place, they will not be justified in facilitating, nor will they be under any obligation to facilitate, the further development of the Jewish National Home by immigration regardless of the wishes of the Arab population.

Land Transfers

16. The Administration of Palestine is required under Article 6 of the Mandate, 'while ensuring that the rights and position of other sections of the population are not prejudiced,' to encourage 'close settlement by Jews on the land,' and no restriction has been imposed hitherto on the transfer of land from Arabs to Jews. The Reports of several expert Commissions have indicated that, owing to the natural growth of the Arab population and the steady sale in recent years of Arab land to Jews, there is now in certain areas no room for further transfers of Arab land, whilst in some other areas such transfers of land must be restricted if Arab cultivators are to maintain their existing standard of life and a considerable landless Arab population is not soon to be created. In these circumstances, the High Commissioner will be given general powers to prohibit and regulate transfers of land. These powers will date from the publication of this statement of Policy and the High Commissioner will retain them throughout the transitional period.

17. The policy of the Government will be directed towards the development of the land and the improvement, where possible, of methods of cultivation. In the light of such development it will be open to the High Commissioner, should he be satisfied that the 'rights and position' of the Arab population will be duly preserved, to review and modify any orders passed relating to the prohibition or restriction of the transfer of land.

6: Extracts from the UN General Assembly Resolution on the Future of Palestine (29 November 1947)

The General Assembly,

Having met in special session at the request of the mandatory Power to constitute and instruct a special committee to prepare for the consideration of the question of the future government of Palestine at the second regular session;

Having constituted a Special Committee and instructed it to investigate all questions and issues relevant to the problem of Palestine, and to prepare proposals for the solution of the problem, and

Having received and examined the report of the Special Committee (document A/364) including a number of unanimous recommendations and a plan of partition with economic union approved by the majority of the Special Committee,

Considers that the present situation in Palestine is one which is likely to impair the general welfare and friendly relations among nations;

Takes note of the declaration by the mandatory Power that it plans to complete its evacuation of Palestine by 1 August 1948;

Recommends to the United Kingdom, as the mandatory Power for Palestine, and to all other Members of the United Nations the adoption and implementation, with regard to the future government of Palestine, of the Plan of Partition with Economic Union set out below; . . .

Plan of Partition with Economic Union

A. TERMINATION OF MANDATE, PARTITION AND INDEPENDENCE

1. The Mandate for Palestine shall terminate as soon as possible but in any case not later than 1 August 1948.

2. The armed forces of the mandatory Power shall be progressively withdrawn from Palestine, the withdrawal to be completed as soon as possible but in any case not later than 1 August 1948.

The Mandatory Power shall advise the Commission, as far in advance as possible, of its intention to terminate the Mandate and to evacuate each area.

The mandatory Power shall use its best endeavours to ensure that an area situated in the territory of the Jewish State, including a seaport and hinterland adequate to provide facilities for a substantial immigration, shall be evacuated at the earliest possible date and in any event not later than 1 February 1948.

3. Independent Arab and Jewish States and the Special International Regime for the City of Jerusalem ... shall come into existence in Palestine two months after the evacuation of the armed forces of the mandatory Power has been completed but in any case not later than 1 October 1948...

4. The period between the adoption by the General Assembly of its recommendation on the question of Palestine and the establishment of the independence of the Arab and Jewish States shall be a transitional period.

B. STEPS PREPARATORY TO INDEPENDENCE

1. A Commission shall be set up consisting of one representative of each of five Member States. The Members represented on the Commission shall be elected by the General Assembly on as broad a basis, geographically and otherwise, as possible.

2. The administration of Palestine shall, as the mandatory Power withdraws its armed forces, be progressively turned over to the Commission, which shall act in conformity with the recommendations of the General Assembly, under the guidance of the Security Council. The mandatory Power shall to the fullest possible extent co-ordinate its plans for withdrawal with the plans of the Commission to take over and administer areas which have been evacuated...

3. On its arrival in Palestine the Commission shall proceed to carry out measures for the establishment of the frontiers of the Arab and Jewish States and the City of Jerusalem in accordance with the general lines of the recommendations of the General Assembly on the partition of Palestine...

Provisional Councils

4. The Commission, after consultation with the democratic parties and other public organizations of the Arab and Jewish States, shall select and establish in each State as rapidly as possible a Provisional Council of Government. The activities of both the Arab and Jewish Provisional Councils of Government shall be carried out under the general direction of the Commission.

If by 1 April 1948 a Provisional Council of Government cannot be selected for either of the States, or, if selected, cannot carry out its functions, the Commission shall communicate that fact to the Security Council for such action with respect to that State as the Security Council may deem proper, and to the Secretary–General for communication to the Members of the United Nations.

5. Subject to the provisions of these recommendations during the transitional period the Provisional Councils of Government, acting under the Commission, shall have full authority in the areas under their control, including authority over matters of immigration and land regulation.

6. The Provisional Council of Government of each State, acting under the Commission, shall progressively receive from the Commission full responsibility for the administration of that State in the period between the termination of the Mandate and the establishment of the State's independence.

7. The Commission shall instruct the Provisional Councils of Government of both the Arab and Jewish States, after their formation, to proceed to the establishment of administrative organs of government, central and local.

Armed Forces

8. The Provisional Council of Government of each State shall, within the shortest time possible, recruit an armed militia from the residents of that State, sufficient in number to maintain internal order and to prevent frontier clashes.

This armed militia in each State shall, for operational purposes, be under the command of Jewish or Arab officers resident in that State, but general political and military control, including the choice of the militia's High Command, shall be exercised by the Commission.

Elections

9. The Provisional Council of Government of each State shall, not later than two months after the withdrawal of the armed forces of the mandatory Power, hold elections to the Constituent Assembly which shall be conducted on democratic lines.

The election regulations in each State shall be drawn up by the Provisional Council of Government and approved by the Commission.

Qualified voters for each State for this election shall be persons over eighteen years of age who are: (a) Palestinian citizens residing in that State and (b) Arabs and Jews residing in the State, although not Palestinian citizens, who, before voting, have signed a notice of intention to become citizens of such State.

Arabs and Jews residing in the City of Jerusalem who have signed a notice of intention to become citizens, the Arabs of the Arab State and the Jews of the Jewish State, shall be entitled to vote in the Arab and Jewish States respectively.

Women may vote and be elected to the Constituent Assemblies.

During the transitional period no Jew shall be permitted to establish residence in the area of the proposed Arab State, and no Arab shall be permitted to establish residence in the area of the proposed Jewish State, except by special leave of the Commission.

Democratic Constitutions

10. The Constituent Assembly of each State shall draft a democratic constitution for its State and choose a provisional government to succeed the Provisional Council of Government appointed by the Commission. The constitutions of the States shall embody chapters 1 and 2 of the Declaration provided for in section C below and include *inter alia* provisions for:

(a) Establishing in each State a legislative body elected by universal suffrage and by secret ballot on the basis of proportional representation, and an executive body responsible to the legislature;

(b) Settling all international disputes in which the State may be involved by peaceful means in such a manner that international peace and security, and justice, are not endangered;

(c) Accepting the obligation of the State to refrain in its international relations from the threat or use of force against the territorial integrity or political independence of any State, or in any other manner inconsistent with the purposes of the United Nations;

(d) Guaranteeing to all persons equal and non-discriminatory rights in civil, political, economic and religious matters and the enjoyment of human rights and fundamental freedoms, including freedom of religion, language, speech and publication, education assembly and association;

(e) Preserving freedom of transit and visit for all residents and citizens of the other State in Palestine and the City of Jerusalem, subject to considerations of national security, provided that each State shall control residence within its borders...

Transitional Administration

12. During the period between the adoption of the recommendations on the question of Palestine by the General Assembly and the termination of the Mandate, the mandatory Power in Palestine shall maintain full responsibility for administration in areas from which it has not withdrawn its armed forces. The Commission shall assist the mandatory Power in the carrying out of these functions. Similarly the mandatory Power shall co-operate with the Commission in the execution of its functions.

13. With a view to ensuring that there shall be continuity in the functioning of administrative services and that, on the withdrawal of the armed forces of the mandatory Power, the whole administration shall be in charge of the Provisional Councils and the Joint Economic Board, respectively, acting under the Commission, there shall be a progressive transfer, from the mandatory Power to the Commission, of responsibility for all the functions of government, including that of maintaining law and order in the areas from which the forces of the mandatory Power have been withdrawn.

14. The Commission shall be guided in its activities by the recommendations of the General Assembly and by such instructions as the Security Council may consider necessary to issue.

The measures taken by the Commission, within the recommendations of the General Assembly, shall become immediately effective unless the Commission has previously received contrary instructions from the Security Council.

The Commission shall render periodic monthly progress reports, or more frequently if desirable, to the Security Council.

15. The Commission shall make its final report to the next regular session of the General Assembly and to the Security Council simultaneously...

7: UN Security Council Resolution 242 (22 November 1967)

The Security Council ...

1. *Affirms* that the fulfilment of Charter principles requires the establishment of a just and lasting peace in the Middle East which should include the application of both the following principles:

(i) Withdrawal of Israeli armed forces from territories occupied in the recent conflict;

(ii) Termination of all claims or states of belligerency and respect for and acknowledgement of the sovereignty, territorial integrity and political independence of every State in the area and their right to live in peace within secure and recognized boundaries free from threats or acts of force,

2. *Affirms further* the necessity

(a) For guaranteeing freedom of navigation through international waterways in the area;

(b) For achieving a just settlement of the refugee problem;

(c) For guaranteeing the territorial inviolability and political independence of every State in the area, through measures including the establishment of demilitarized zones.

3. *Requests* the Secretary-General to designate a Special Representative to proceed to the Middle East to establish and maintain contacts with the States concerned in order to promote agreement and assist efforts to achieve a peaceful and accepted settlement in accordance with the provisions and principles in this resolution;

4. *Requests* the Secretary-General to report to the Security Council on the progress of the efforts of the Special Representative as soon as possible.

8: UN Security Council Resolution 338 (22 October 1973)

The Security Council,

1. *Calls upon* all parties to the present fighting to cease all firing and terminate all military activity immediately, not later than 12 hours after the moment of the adoption of the decision, in the positions they now occupy;

2. *Calls upon* the parties concerned to start immediately after the ceasefire the implementation of Security Council Resolution 242 (1967) in all of its parts;

3. *Decides that,* immediately and concurrently with the ceasefire, negotiations start between the parties concerned under appropriate auspices aimed at establishing a just and durable peace in the Middle East.

9: Extracts from European Community Declaration issued in Venice (13 June 1980)

4... the time has come to promote the recognition and implementation of the two principles universally accepted by the international community: the right to existence and to security of all the states in the region, including Israel, and justice for all the peoples which implies the recognition of the legitimate rights of the Palestinian people.

5. All of the countries in the area are entitled to live in peace within secure, recognised and guaranteed borders. The necessary guarantees for a peace settlement should be provided by the United Nations by a decision of the Security Council and, if necessary, on the basis of other mutually agreed procedures. The Nine declared that they are prepared to participate within the framework of a comprehensive settlement in a system of concrete and binding international guarantees, including (guarantees) on the ground.

6. A just solution must finally be found to the Palestinian problem, which is not simply one of refugees. The Palestinian people, which is conscious of existing as such, must be placed in a position, by an appropriate process defined within the framework of the comprehensive peace settlement, to exercise fully its right to self-determination.

7. The achievement of these objectives requires the involvement and support of all the parties concerned in the peace settlement which the Nine are endeavouring to promote in keeping with the principles formulated in the declaration referred to above. These principles apply to all the parties concerned, and thus the Palestinian people, and to the PLO, which will have to be associated with the negotiations.

8. The Nine recognise the special importance of the role played by the question of Jerusalem for all the parties concerned. The Nine stress that they will not accept any unilateral initiative designed to change the status of Jerusalem and that any agreement on the city's status should guarantee freedom of access for everyone to the holy places.

9. The Nine stress the need for Israel to put an end to the territorial occupation which it has maintained since the conflict of 1967, as it has done for part of Sinai. They are deeply convinced that the Israeli settlements constitute a serious obstacle to the peace process in the Middle East. The Nine consider that these settlements, as well as modifications in population and property in the occupied Arab territories, are illegal under international law.

10. Concerned as they are to put an end to violence, the Nine consider that only the renunciation of force or the threatened use of force by all the parties can create a climate of confidence in the area, and constitute a basic element for a comprehensive settlement of the conflict in the Middle East.

11. The Nine have decided to make the necessary contacts with all the parties concerned. The objective of these contacts would be to ascertain the position of the various parties with respect to the principles set out in this declaration and in the light of the result of this consultation process to determine the form which such an initiative on their part could take.

Further Reading

£

Britain and the Gulf Crisis (Aspects of Britain).
ISBN 0 11 701734 5.   HMSO   1993   5.00

*The Israel–Arab Reader: A Documentary History
of the Middle East Conflict.* Edited by Laquer & Rubin.
ISBN 0 14 022588 9.   Penguin 1985   7.50

*A Peace to End All Peace: Creating the Modern
Middle East 1914–22.* David Fromkin.
ISBN 0 14 015445 0.   Penguin 1991   7.99

*The Politics of Partition: King Abdullah, the Zionists
and Palestine 1921–51.* Avi Shlaim.
ISBN 0 19 285223 X.   Oxford   1990   7.95

Index

Printed in the UK for HMSO.
Dd.0296535, 6/93, C30, 51-2423, 5673, 247509.

THE ANNUAL PICTURE

BRITAIN HANDBOOK

The annual picture of Britain is provided by *Britain: An Official Handbook* - the forty-fourth edition will be published early in 1993. It is the unrivalled reference book about Britain, packed with information and statistics on every facet of British life.

With a circulation of over 20,000 worldwide, it is essential for libraries, educational institutions, business organisations and individuals needing easy access to reliable and up-to-date information, and is supported in this role by its sister publication, *Current Affairs: A Monthly Survey*.

Approx. 500 pages; 24 pages of colour illustrations; 16 maps; diagrams and tables throughout the text; and a statistical section. Price £19·50.

Buyers of Britain 1993: An Official Handbook *have the opportunity of a year's subscription to* Current Affairs *at 25 per cent off the published price of £35·80. They will also have the option of renewing their subscription next year at the same discount. Details in each copy of* Handbook, *from HMSO Publications Centre and at HMSO bookshops (see back of title page).*

CI159